12

Days Out
With God

12 Days Out With God

A Hands-On Guide to Rediscovering God

Chris Gidney & Mike Elcome

ZONDERVAN™

GRAND RAPIDS, MICHIGAN 49530 USA

We want to hear from you. Please send your comments about this book to us in care of zreview@zondervan.com. Thank you.

ZONDERVAN™

12 Days Out with God
Copyright © 2003 by Chris Gidney and Mike Elcome

Requests for information should be addressed to:
Zondervan, *Grand Rapids, Michigan 49530*

ISBN 0-310-24885-X

Interior design by Beth Shagene

Illustrations by Lyn Boyer

Printed in the United States of America

03 04 05 06 07 08 09 /❖ DC/ 10 9 8 7 6 5 4 3 2 1

Contents

Preface

Do you ever wish you could just reach out beyond all the complexities of life and simply touch God? I do! He would answer my searching questions, listen to my worries and bring reassurance that in life's most difficult moments he is still in control.

But I can't reach God on the phone or even drop him an email. What I have to rely on is the Bible, my own experience of God and the understanding of others. Sometimes though, this still doesn't seem enough. I was made to live in a physical world, and I want to know if there is a way of knowing God 'in the flesh' too.

All the obstacles of life caused me to stop one day and really question whether God was still interested in me. I got bogged down by the jargon at church and needed something more than just a song and a sermon. But could I find God beyond church? When I sat down and shared some of these thoughts with my minister, Mike, I was surprised to find that he was just as keen as I was to meet God in a new way.

It wasn't that we had lost our faith; God was still very real to us. It wasn't that our faith had become unrelated to our everyday lives; we realized that we relied on him now more than ever. It was simply that having known God for so long it was as if our relationship with him had gone stale. Like a lake that had become stagnant when the flow of the river running into it had stopped, or the car that couldn't race any more because it had gone too many miles, so our relationship with God was just managing to creak along, but the 'spark' had gone.

Where was all the excitement of discovering God for the first time? Why had all our original zeal for him disappeared? Like a human heart that had become clogged with the fatty deposits of cholesterol, our experience of God had become congested. What we needed most of all was a spiritual holiday, a way of rediscovering God in a new and tangible way. We needed a physical reminder that God was still in control, that he possessed the many qualities that made him God, and above all that he still loved us.

'If you were looking for God, where would you go?' I asked Mike one lunchtime.

'I'd go to the gardens,' came his reply. 'I'd like to see if I can find God in the bigger picture of creation.'

'I would look for him in an art gallery,' I suggested. 'I'd like to see whether paintings can help me understand my relationship with God.'

'Then let's do it!' Mike said as he leapt up for action.

And so, out of a necessity to see if we could find God beyond our normal church activities, the Spiritual Travellers Guide series was born.

We found that we *could* meet God at the theme park, by the river, on a journey, in the art gallery, and even while shopping!

We discovered that our days out with God proved that he is actively involved and interested in every part of our lives no matter how big or small. He cares deeply about how we feel and what we do, and he wants to have an on-going relationship with us. In fact God desires to become so close to us that he wants us to feel we could almost reach out and touch him. The only problem is ourselves, because half the time we don't really believe he wants to spend time with us.

'There are too many other important things going on in the world,' we say. 'Why should the Creator of the World be bothered about little me with all my failings?' we ask.

This book shows you that wherever you go, God will be there. Not out of duty, but out of choice. He is available to you today. Indeed, he wants to have a day out relaxing and conversing with you. Can you believe it?

Introduction

In a rut?

Wondering where God is?

Feeling empty inside?

Want to get closer to God?

Then take a break and discover God in a new and dynamic way!

With this practical, enlightening and entertaining book, you'll embark on a series of exciting adventures that lead you to find God in unexpected places.

Explaining that this is not a book to *read* but to *do*, an experienced minister and a showbiz author take you on an exciting journey to deepen your faith. In a fresh and unique way, they lead you on a practical pathway of self-discovery and an understanding of your personal relationship with God.

The twelve days out with God can be enjoyed with a friend or individually. Each has been tested not only by us but by a group of field testers. And each is designed to help you find God in your everyday life and beyond the walls of the church. Discover the God of history, the God of creation and the God of relationships. Can you really find God at the theme park, in a library and at the cemetery?

The series of days can be done at your own pace. You could do one a month or one a year; it is entirely up to you to decide. Each day out is set in a very user-friendly style and every adventure has a spiritual aim, with tangible ideas ready to be put into action. It contains practical exercises, stories, questions, Bible verses, prayers and suggestions of how to turn your new discovery of God into a daily reality.

God loves sharing in our everyday experiences, and he is ready to have a day out enjoying your company. Why not slip on your walking shoes, button up your coat and join us for a journey with a difference? Are you coming . . . ?

How to Use This Book

Don't skip this section, as it's the key
to making the book work for you.

Finding God

It might surprise you to know that despite his apparent absence sometimes, God isn't in the habit of hiding. In fact his promise 'seek and you will find' means that he is always near. But are we always accessible to him? Choosing to spend a day out with God will take you away from all the hustle and bustle of life, and will lead you to encounter God by 'doing'. Each chapter is designed as an activity that will allow you to start thinking about God in a new way, and then will lead you to discover God in a new way. It is based on the passionate belief that God can be found in this world, and that he is always willing to share himself with you.

Choice

Although the chapters are arranged in a useful order, you can choose which 'Day out with God' to do on any particular day. In this way the chapter will meet your own particular need, your feelings and desires on that day. In other words, choose the chapter you want to do each day, according to your mood.

Progression

This manual is designed to involve you in a process of spiritual discovery that arises directly out of a personal experience. Thus it is better to work through each 'Day out with God' starting at the beginning and avoiding the temptation to go straight to the reflective bits or the questions. Like all good travel directions, there is a deliberate progression within each chapter, so it's best to avoid picking at odd sections in a random kind of way. Some of the chapters work straight through from start to finish; in others you may be directed to flip backwards and forwards as you make your discoveries.

   If you find yourself being drawn to different questions and different reflections than those that are suggested, that's fine. Our ideas are neither compulsory, nor are they the only possibilities. Use the questions that you find appropriate, helpful and those that open up new spiritual insights for you. As you answer the questions, try and apply your discoveries to your own life.

Do I Have to Do Them All?

You may find that some of the chapters in this book work better for you than others. In fact, some may not work at all! That's not a problem. Quite possibly you will be asked to go to some places that you are not particularly interested in or to answer questions that may not 'push the right buttons' for you. Nevertheless, we would encourage you to stick with it. You will be amazed how you will eventually discover *something* that you would probably have missed had you opted out. Try and do all of the twelve days if you can, but bear in mind that this is not an exam.

Is It Hard Work?

Like your bank account, what you get out of this book will be directly related to what you put into it. For the best results we recommend that you approach it with a sense of enthusiasm and commitment. After all, there is often more fulfilment and payback from achieving something that demands your hard work and sweat. But it can be great fun too!

Honesty

For this book to work for you, approach each session with an open mind. It's better not to decide what you will find before you start looking. And as you answer the questions, don't be afraid of being honest in your answers. If we were truly honest, we would acknowledge that we don't actually want God near us all the time. In our darker moments, we think it's easier to keep him on the sidelines rather than to allow ourselves the embarrassment of imagining him standing nearby. However, these adventures help us acknowledge that God is everywhere and wants to be involved in our lives. Someone once said, 'God is never disillusioned with us, because he never had any illusions about us in the first place!'

Self-Discovery

You may be surprised just how many of the questions are about self-discovery and how this relates to your relationship with God. There are no right or wrong answers, just things you will notice or that have jumped out at you. This can be a very fulfilling part of your day out, like being in a spiritual gym. You may feel tired at the end of it, but exhilarated as well.

On Your Own or with Others?

Most of the activities in this book will work either on your own or with others. They can be light-hearted and fun, but it is up to you to decide whether you want to make this a more individual and personal experience or whether you want to involve a friend. You could even try doing some chapters as a small group activity, but don't feel you need to share all your answers with others.

Unearthing Negatives

As life is made up of both light and dark, so some of your discoveries may be tough going, unwelcome, uncomfortable and even make you feel quite low. Don't despair! Sometimes it's more important to recognize and work on the issues we are struggling with rather than simply to focus on those we have already conquered. This book gives you an opportunity to talk to God about the downside of your life and perhaps begin to turn negatives into positives.

Personal Diary

This expedition will be unique to you. Your personal *12 Days Out with God* will become a useful scrapbook or diary to refer back to in future years. You will be able to remind yourself of the discoveries you made, see how your views may have changed and be amazed at how your walk with God has developed. The Spiritual Notepad in each chapter can be completed as you go along, noting significant things as they come to you.

Take It Easy

Whatever you do, don't rush. This book is not a short-term project to be completed in a week. It is more like a long hot bubbly bath than a quick shower. Take your time; otherwise you may not discover all that is hidden and waiting to be found. Your aim is not to get from A to Z in supersonic time. Take it slowly enough to stop, look, listen and take in as much as possible of what is to be seen and found on the way. You can choose to do one day out a week, a month or a year!

Don't Feel Guilty

If you find you are unable to give as much time to each adventure as you hoped, don't worry. God knows the sort of pressurized world you live in, and you can always repeat the day out on another occasion. You will probably find yourself amazed at the different answers you give a second time around.

Finding Time

The whole point of this book is to encourage you to take time out to discover God. You may think you are far too busy to tackle any of the chapters, but clearing space to meet your own needs is vital. When you actually get around to making time, you will be surprised at just how good it is. You're worth it!

Your Personal 'Road Map'

Any traveller needs to take a break to recharge their batteries and check their route from time to time. So it is that each adventure has ten 'stopping points' along the way where you are asked questions, given thoughts to reflect on, prayers to pray or things to do in order to make your 'Day Out with God' come to life. Here is a sort of road map to show where the twists and turns of each expedition will take you. Have you packed your spiritual compass?

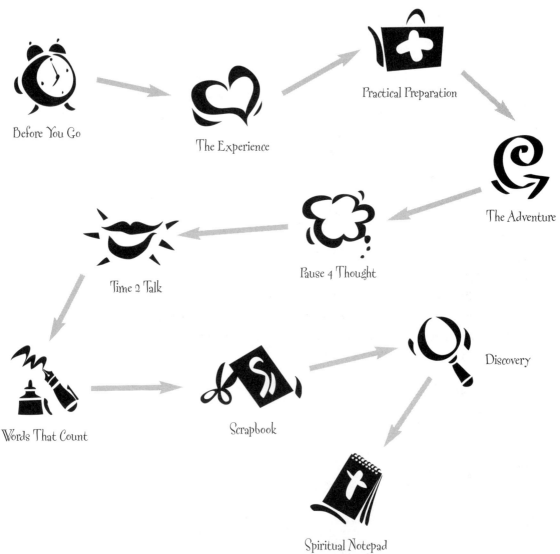

Before You Go

The Experience

Practical Preparation

The Adventure

Pause 4 Thought

Time 2 Talk

Words That Count

Scrapbook

Discovery

Spiritual Notepad

Measure Up

Just like weighing yourself when you arrive at the gym, it might be useful to take a 'spot check' on where you are spiritually before you begin. You can then re-analyze this at the end of your experiences to see how much and where you may have gained more knowledge about yourself and your relationship with God.

On a scale of 1 to 10, put a ring around where you would consider yourself at the moment in . . .

Your personal day to day relationship with God:

    1   2   3   4   5   6   7   8   9   10
Low   High

Your prayer life:

    1   2   3   4   5   6   7   8   9   10
Low   High

Your measure of faith and trust:

    1   2   3   4   5   6   7   8   9   10
Low   High

Your knowledge of your inner self:

    1   2   3   4   5   6   7   8   9   10
Low   High

Your general spiritual fitness:

    1   2   3   4   5   6   7   8   9   10
Low   High

Confidence in your ability to get closer to God:

    1   2   3   4   5   6   7   8   9   10
Low   High

Just for You

As you will see, each section in this guidebook includes plenty of
blank spaces. This is *your* space, an on-going scrapbook for you to
write, draw or stick in souvenirs of your activity. We will give you
some ideas as to what to do on this page, but don't let these limit you.
The space is *yours* and you can be as creative as you like!

We're Off!

So now you've bought the guide, why not take out your calendar and
plan your first adventure?

Come on . . . what are you waiting for?

Let's go!

1. Taking a Journey

Steps of Discovery

Visit to:	Date:

Before You Go

We all go on journeys. Some are short and essential, while many are repetitive and simply the means to an end. Occasionally, however, the excitement is not only to be found in the place we are going to, but also in the process of getting there. As a child it was like that going on holiday. My parents did all they could to make the actual journey fun, including at one stage giving us a little wrapped present to open every half hour, eliminating the 'Are we nearly there?' syndrome almost completely. And the first occasion that I went on a journey by plane, the excitement of that experience was almost as good as enjoying the final destination.

Christians have a long history of experiencing the joy and the spiritual element of travel through years of sharing in pilgrimages. The English poet Geoffrey Chaucer, who lived from about 1340 to 1400, wrote about pilgrimages in his famous *Canterbury Tales*. These are stories of pilgrims travelling to Canterbury, particularly going to see the place where Thomas Becket was killed. Such pilgrimages were not all serious – far from it! Indeed, they could be great fun. There were hostels strategically placed along the route, and pilgrims travelled in small groups, talking, singing and stopping at places of spiritual interest. This combination of relaxation and spirituality can serve as a helpful model for our first day out with God.

Practical Preparation

☆ Choose a place to visit that will mean making a journey involving at least two forms of transport in which you are a passenger.

☆ Your chosen destination should be somewhere you would like to go to, but a place that you are not too familiar with. Somewhere about an hour away from your starting point would be ideal.

☆ Before you go, glance through the questions you are going to be asked about your journey.

☆ There are many different aspects of a journey described in the next section, but not all of these will be relevant to the journey you take. Feel free to ignore those that do not relate.

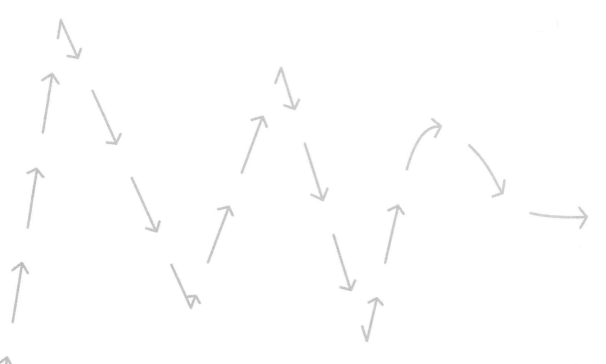

The Experience

☆ There are two main parts to this experience. The first looks at the actual journey you take. The second invites you to take a closer look at its meaning for your life.

☆ Use the first part of the Adventure section to record your journey as you go along, noting the twists and turns and the ups and downs of travel.

☆ On your arrival, find somewhere to go and sit down with a drink. Take some time to reflect on your journey and its spiritual implications.

☆ The closing part of the chapter can be done as you travel back home.

The Adventure

*H*ere we look at the various features of your journey as you go along, then in the next section we will see how these can be applied to your spiritual journey.

Waiting and Delays

☆ Make a note here of any experiences of waiting or being delayed that you encounter.

☆ If you missed a bus, a train or any connection, write that experience down here.

☆ What feelings and thoughts do you experience as you have to wait?

Maps and Timetables

☆ What travel directions or timetables are part of your journey?

Getting Lost, Going the Wrong Way and Detours
☆ If you get lost or go the wrong way, record what happened.

☆ If, in any part of your journey, you make a detour, note the details here.

☆ What does it feel like when you make a detour?

Keeping Your Eyes Open
☆ What do you observe as you travel that especially makes an impact on you?

Instructions
☆ As you travel you are bombarded with notices, signs and instructions. Make a note of some of them here.

Advertising

☆ The advertisers see travellers as a sitting target for their messages. Record one or two advertising messages that particularly catch your attention.

Entertaining and Eating

☆ How would you normally keep yourself entertained as you travel?

☆ Are you planning to eat anything on your journey?

Self-Discovery

☆ What are you learning about yourself on this journey?

Problems and Frustrations

☆ Are you encountering any problems, frustrations or obstacles that make your journey more difficult?

Risks and Dangers

☆ If you find you have to take a risk during your journey then record that here.

☆ Are there any notable dangers you find yourself facing as you travel?

Fellow Travellers

☆ Think about those who are sharing your journey with you. Are these other travellers a help or a hindrance to you and your journey?

☆ Are there times when the best thing to do is follow the crowd?

Luggage

☆ What luggage are you carrying with you?

☆ Is that presenting you with any difficulties?

Journey Speeds and Tiredness

☆ Record the speeds at which you think you are travelling as you use different modes of transport.

1.

2.

3.

4.

☆ Which speed do you find the easiest? Why?

☆ Is travelling an experience that, at any point, makes you feel tired?

Checks

☆ If anyone checks up on you during your journey, jot that down here.

☆ What does it feel like to have someone checking up on you?

Pause 4 Thought

Brother Lawrence was a monk in a seventeenth century monastery. He coined the phrase 'practicing the presence of God'. When he died his Abbé said of him: 'The good brother found God everywhere . . . as much when he was repairing shoes, as when he was praying.' Whether still in his bed, or on the move, Brother Lawrence knew God was right beside him.

Travelling, which is such as essential part of life today, is a great place to start practicing the presence of God. When you arrive at your destination, look for somewhere to sit down and reflect on the following questions as you consider your own life's journey

Waiting and Delays

☆ Like it or not, interruptions are often features of a journey. They can leave us very frustrated. What kinds of delays have you discovered in your experience of life and of God?

☆ The Bible often uses the idea of waiting in a very positive way. Even the disciples had to wait for the coming of God's Spirit. How can you make the idea of waiting a constructive one?

Maps and Timetables

☆ Sometimes maps and timetables are not only helpful, but essential, especially in an unknown place. Some people find maps easy to use, while others really struggle with them. What kind of maps do you have for your faith journey?

☆ How easy do you find it to read the map?

Getting Lost, Going the Wrong Way and Detours

☆ Sometimes it feels as if our lives are going in the wrong direction, caught up in a diversion or going nowhere at all. At times we may feel as if we are travelling down a road that leads to a dead end! Do you feel lost in any way today?

☆ What do you do when your life goes off track?

☆ Sometimes you can opt out of your journey for a time, maybe to rest or to go and do something else. Do you ever feel that you have opted out of your journey with God?

Keeping Your Eyes Open

☆ What observations have you made about the journey of life so far?

☆ Have any of those things surprised you?

Instructions

☆ Do you feel that God has personally given you any instructions for your life? If so, what do you believe they are?

Advertising

☆ Are there images or messages that you feel you have been forced to experience in life, whether you want to or not?

☆ If so, how do you deal with these unwanted invasions?

Entertaining and Eating

☆ What sustains you on your journey through life?

☆ How important to you is having fun and enjoying what you do?

Problems and Frustrations

☆ What do you feel are the two biggest problems you are facing at the moment?

    1.

    2.

☆ How might you begin to overcome these?

    1.

    2.

Risks and Dangers

☆ What is the biggest risk you have taken so far in your life?

☆ Do you regret taking it?

☆ Are there any dangers on your horizon that you feel could be a threat to you? How realistic are your fears?

Fellow-Travellers

☆ Make a note of the most significant people accompanying you on your journey of life at the moment, perhaps just using their initials. Some may be those who are of help to you, others could be a hindrance. Try and write down what difference the people you have included are making to your journey at the moment.

Luggage

☆ What heavy baggage are you carrying through your life?

☆ If you would like the weight you carry to be lessened, how might you enable that to happen?

Journey Speeds and Tiredness

☆ How would you describe the pace of your life at the moment?

☆ Are you happy with that?

☆ Do you find that life often makes you very tired?

☆ Is that inevitable, or is there something you can do about it?

☆ What is the most energizing part of your life today?

Checks

☆ Do you ever feel like anyone is checking up on you? Who does this?

☆ Do you wish there were more or fewer checks on you? Why?

Destinations

☆ Think for a moment about the chosen destination of your journey today. Why did you choose this destination? Was it so obvious that there was little choice, or could you have chosen lots of different places to go?

☆ Do you feel that there is a clear destination for your life or does that destination feel uncertain and unknown? Do you feel that you have any choices to make in the matter?

☆ Does it make any difference to your life whether or not you have a specific idea of where you are heading?

☆ Do you think that the future of your journey is in your own hands? Or does it feel dependent on forces and events from outside over which you have no control? Or is it somewhere in between?

Time 2 Talk

Why not talk to God today as you travel back home? If you're not alone, you could write out your thoughts, or converse quietly in your mind.

Talk to God about the aspects of your journey that have set you thinking.

Talk about what you see, and about your life.

Talk about the thoughts and feelings you have about your own life's journey.

Talk about the stage in your journey you feel you have reached so far.

Next time you go for a walk, try talking and walking at the same time.

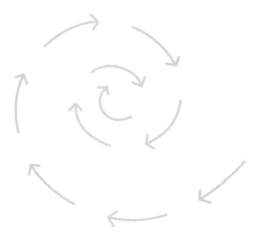

Discovery

☆ What are the three most important things you have learned about yourself so far in your journey through life?

1.

2.

3.

☆ Were there any other discoveries you made about your various journeys today?

Words That Count

Words that refer to some form of travel are commonly used in the Bible to describe faith. Jesus often challenged people to respond to him with the words 'Follow me', and one of the first labels given to Christians was 'followers of the way'.

Here are some more words with a journeying theme:

> 'I am going there to prepare a place for you. And if I go and prepare a place for you, I will come back and take you to be with me, that you also may be where I am. You know the way to the place where I am going.'
>
> Thomas said to him, 'Lord, we don't know where you are going, so how can we know the way?'
>
> Jesus answered, 'I am the way and the truth and the life . . .'
>
> *John 14:2–6*

Spiritual Notepad

☆ Try expressing the spiritual journey of your life up until now in the form of a simple map. There may well be twists and turns, diversions and no-through roads, as well as times when the road has been relatively straight.

☆ After you have drawn your map, try to imagine what the immediate journey ahead will be like.

Scrapbook

Stick here some mementos of your journey, such as a map, a ticket or a public transport timetable.

2. The Art Gallery

Reflections of God

Visit to:	Date:

Before You Go

It was in war-torn Beirut, Lebanon, that Church of England envoy Terry Waite was kidnapped by the extremist group Hezbollah. From January 1987 people around the world began to hope and pray for his safety and release.

Interestingly, it was a British housewife living in Bedford who gave Terry the hope he needed. Joy Brodier not only joined in the prayers for Terry that were included in the regular service of her church, but she also decided to do something more.

When Joy came across a postcard depicting the seventeenth century preacher John Bunyan imprisoned for his religious beliefs, it gave her an idea. She purchased the postcard that featured a stained-glass window showing John Bunyan in his cell, writing the famous *Pilgrim's Progress.*

On the back, Joy wrote a simple message for Terry: 'People everywhere are praying for you.' She signed it but didn't know how to address it. Finally she wrote: 'Terry Waite, c/o Hezbollah (Party of God), Beirut, Lebanon.' At the post office the clerk looked at it and then charged Joy the normal rate for an airmail postcard to Beirut.

During the following three years, some could not believe that Terry was still alive, others hoped against hope. In 1991 word finally came that Terry Waite was being freed. When Terry landed on British soil in November, he spoke to the waiting journalists and TV cameras. As a worn-down but glad Terry spoke of his 1,763 days in prison, he mentioned his thanks to those who had been praying for him, and then he spoke of a postcard. It was the only piece of mail that had reached him in nearly five years, and its picture was a great source of comfort.

Art can be a comfort to us too. God has given people the skills to draw, paint and sculpt in ways that can not only reflect the world around us, but bring spiritual insight too.

Practical Preparation

☆ Choose a local art gallery that is likely to have a wide range of exhibition material. (If you are unable to get to one near you, consider taking a virtual tour of an online gallery. We suggest www.nationalgallery.org.uk or www.nga.gov.)

☆ Bring a camera to take photos of pieces of art that impress you, but check with the gallery first to find out if this is allowed. Some authorize this only at off-peak times.

☆ Be prepared to purchase small souvenirs or postcards.

☆ Decide if you would like a guided tour. This can be a little restrictive, but can help focus on a select number of pictures.

☆ Pray that God will open your mind as your adventure begins.

☆ Plan two hours to look around at leisure and allow some extra time to answer the questions.

☆ As soon as you arrive, spend an hour exploring the gallery. Acquaint yourself with the type of paintings it displays, and make a note of any that you are particularly attracted to or repelled by.

☆ Choose three paintings to look at in more detail. One should be of Christ, one that represents some form of evil and another of a landscape or seascape.

☆ If you are sharing the experience with a friend, arrange a time to meet up and discuss your findings.

The Adventure

Picture of Christ

☆ How is Christ portrayed?

☆ How does the artist convey a sense of the spiritual in the painting?

☆ What would he be saying to you if the picture could speak?

☆ Is this how you imagine Christ to be?

☆ What would you say to Christ if the picture could hear?

☆ Is there anything else this painting says to you?

Picture of Evil

☆ What type of evil do you see in this image?

☆ What frightens you about this picture?

☆ What effect does it have on you?

☆ How would you take a stand against this evil?

☆ Is God represented anywhere in this painting?

☆ What questions does the picture raise for you?

☆ Do you make any other observations?

Picture of a Landscape or Seascape

☆ What words would you use to describe this painting?

☆ Why were you drawn to it?

☆ What feelings surface as you look at this picture?

☆ What might it be saying to you?

☆ What do you think God feels about the painting?

☆ What do you see of God, the creator in this picture?

Spiritual Notepad

☆ As time allows, choose a painting that represents how you are
feeling. Describe or draw it here.

☆ Why have you chosen this painting?

Pause 4 Thought

God cares about your innermost feelings. Sometimes you can't put into words the pain, confusion, joy or excitement that goes on deep inside. God is able to see the picture that is painted on your soul, and understands the artist within.

Time 2 Talk

☆ Why not thank God that he is still in the process of painting the picture of your life?

☆ What aspects of the picture would you like him to concentrate on?

☆ You can write your prayer below if you like.

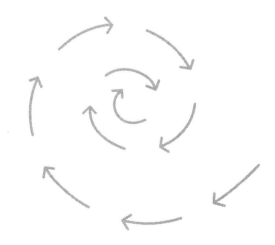

Words That Count

When I consider your heavens,
the work of your fingers,
the moon and the stars
which you have set in place,
what is man,
that you are mindful of him . . . ?

Psalm 8:3–4

Discovery

☆ What aspects of God did you notice at the Gallery today?

☆ Has anything made you 'change tack' today?

Scrapbook

☆ Stick here some memento of your visit.

3. The Museum

History in the Making

Visit to:	Date:

Before You Go

God and history are so closely linked; you could almost say it was . . . his-story.

Our own history goes hand-in-hand with God's, because he walks with us every step of the way. When the psalmist says, 'Surely goodness and love will follow me,' (Psalm 23:6) we realize that it is only when we take time to stop and look back over the shoulder of our lives that we can begin to appreciate how God really was there.

When we take the trouble to look back in time, we can learn so much that will spur us on into the future. Every achievement or mistake we make is a valuable lesson in the stepping stone of life. Forget these at your peril!

Today, as you visit the museum, not only are you going to take a look back, but forwards too, as you make today become tomorrow's history. As you begin to dig up the past, perhaps you will also discover something of God's track record.

Practical Preparation

Choose a museum in your locality that is likely to have a wide range of exhibition material. It should contain human, animal and natural exhibits.(If you are unable to get to one near you, consider taking a virtual tour of an online museum. We suggest www.nhm.ac.uk, natural-history.uoregon.edu/Pages/info.html or www.vmnh.org.)

☆ Bring a camera to take photos of items that impress you, but check first to find out if this is allowed in the museum. Some authorize this only at off-peak times.

☆ Be prepared to purchase small souvenirs or postcards for your scrapbook.

☆ Pray that God will open your mind as your adventure begins.

☆ Try and shut out the world and its worries around you and relax. Take your time!

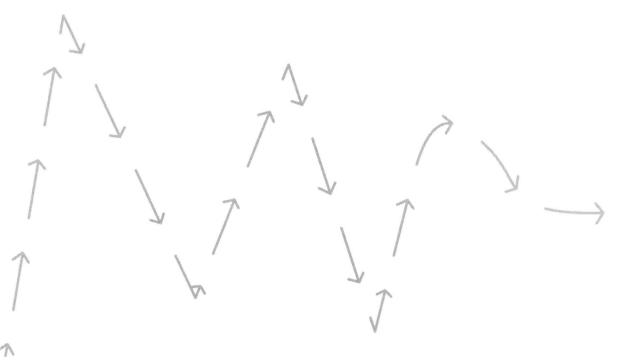

The Experience

☆ Plan two hours to look around at leisure and to answer the questions below as you go.

☆ The adventure is based on three sections, and you can answer them in any order.

☆ Leave some time at the end of your day out to sit down for some refreshment and answer the final set of discovery questions.

☆ If you are doing this with a friend, arrange a time to meet up at the end to compare notes.

The Adventure

Human Exhibit

☆ Find a very old exhibit on display that is connected to humans. What strikes you about this exhibit?

☆ How do you imagine God saw the world at this early date?

☆ How many things can you list that spring to mind of how the world has changed since then?

☆ Do you think God has changed his view of the world since this time?

☆ Is there any evidence of a spiritual dimension to life here?

Animal Exhibit

☆ Find the largest and smallest animal exhibits. Which exhibit strikes you as being the most unusual?

☆ Is there a subject of one of the exhibits that you would be afraid to meet face to face?

☆ Is there an example of an extinct creature?

☆ Why do you think God bothered to make a creature he knew would be extinct one day?

☆ Is there a new discovery for you here?

Natural Exhibit

☆ Are there any views of the earth from space?

☆ Is there anything here that helps you see the world through God's eyes?

☆ Are there any fossils on show? If so, which is the oldest?

☆ Write down any printed words, phrases or quotes that particularly strike you.

☆ Do you imagine that God has created life elsewhere in the universe?

Spiritual Notepad

☆ In your imagination, choose an exhibit that you would like to take home with you to remind you of God. Write or draw a description of the object you have chosen, what it reminds you of and why.

Pause 4 Thought

God was there from the start. He was there from the start with you too.

God has walked each step of the way with you in your life, even when you didn't notice him.

Time 2 Talk

Thank you, God, that you were there from the start.
That you were there the day I was conceived.
The day I was born.
You heard my first word, and went through the gates with me on my
    first day at school.
You sat with me in my exams, and were there at my first job interview.
You were there when I cried and felt pain.
You sat with me when I was lonely.
You were there at my beginning.
You are here with me now.
You will be with me till my journey's end.

                                                    Amen.

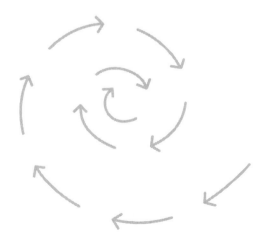

Words That Count

For a thousand years in your sight
are like a day that has just gone by
Psalm 90:4

Discovery

☆ What new aspect of God did you discover at the gallery today?

☆ In what ways has your own viewpoint changed after today's experience?

Scrapbook

☆ Stick here some memento of your visit.

4. In the Gardens

The Designer's Label

Visit to:	Date:

Before You Go

I wonder if disciples often gave Jesus a headache. They often took so long to understand what he was saying, and many times missed the point altogether.

One day Jesus was talking to them on the subject of worry. He was trying to explain that if God was their loving spiritual parent, and if God was committed always to do what was best for them, then it made very little sense to worry about things.

In order to emphasize what he was saying, Jesus pointed to the wild flowers that were growing right by their feet at that very moment. I like to think that he even bent down and picked one, holding it up for all to see. Then Jesus said something like this: 'Isn't that beautiful? Simple, but beautiful. It doesn't have to struggle, worry and fret to be like that. This beauty just happens. It is God-given. And that's all the more remarkable in view of the fact that these flowers won't last for too long. Soon these plants will be cut down and turned into fuel for someone's stove. Yet even so, God looks after each one and gives them their wonderful beauty, shape and colour.'

Then, with the way that he had, Jesus turned to those listening with his challenge. 'And God will look after you in just the same way. If he does it for this flower, surely it's not too hard to see that he will do it for you. So there is no need to worry. Unbelievers worry. That's a natural part of living without faith in God. But this flower says that if you believe you should not always be worrying. There is absolutely no need to be eaten up with anxiety if you have faith in God and put him first.'

And so the flower brings a message from God. You might even say that the flower, in its own way, 'speaks'.

This day out is intended to help you see and hear messages from God, as the plants in the garden 'speak' their own words of spiritual truth just for you. For it really is possible to find God in the gardens you are visiting today.

Practical Preparation

☆ This day out involves finding and visiting public gardens, and spending time there in appreciation, reflection and thought.

☆ It does not really matter what time of the year you go, as each season offers something different. However, you will need to be there for an hour at least, and longer if you like, as you use the ideas and suggestions of this chapter.

☆ If it is possible, be prepared to buy something small at the end of your visit for your scrapbook.

☆ If you are just not able to visit any public gardens, then there are a few other possibilities you could try. You could work through this chapter in your own garden or yard. You could try it in the local garden centre, or with some plant catalogues in front of you. You could even look on the Internet for garden sites, possibly starting with something like www.rhs.org.uk.

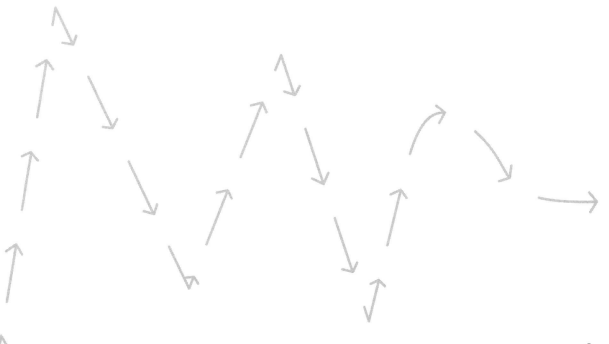

The Experience

☆ Look through the chapter first, before you do anything else.

☆ Then take a slow walk around the gardens to see what you can discover, flipping back and forth over the next pages as you go along.

☆ Find somewhere to sit as you work through the last section.

☆ Visit the shop if there is one to help you with the scrapbook suggestions.

The Adventure

Natural Beauty

☆ People have different ways of understanding creation and evolution, but one thing is clear: God is the architect and creator of our living planet, and here in the gardens we come into close contact with his creation. In the same way that an artist signs a painting to mark it as his, so we believe you can see God's signature in the world he has made. One aspect of that is the existence of natural beauty, which is an expression of God's own character and nature. Find four or five examples of different sorts of things that are particularly attractive to you. Look out for colour, shape and different artistic forms.

1.

2.

3.

4.

5.

☆ Even if you don't have an outstanding track record in art, have a go at drawing one of those examples of natural beauty that you noted above. You could do an outline in the garden now and then complete the picture later.

Variety

☆ Variety in creation is not accidental, but is a reflection of an infinite God. So as you walk, look out for examples of variety and diversity. You will probably find that you experience these through all your senses, that is through sight, sound, smell, feeling and even taste. Find some examples of different sorts of things that are particularly attractive to you. Look out for colour, shape and different artistic forms.

Variety you have seen:

Variety as smelled:

Variety as heard:

☆ If you were a plant, what plant would you like to be? And where would you choose to be planted?

Design

☆ The fact that this universe looks in so many places as if it has been designed, rather than being the result of chance, is a real problem to the complete atheist. So wander around the gardens and see if you can find any evidence that points to this world being made by a Designer, rather than luck, chance or an accident. Either describe or draw some of the design features you have come across.

☆ Did anything remind you today of the fact that people so often copy nature in one way or another?

73

Cooperation

☆ The fact that all living beings work together in an environmental ecosystem again points to an overall plan by one who is a God of order. Try and find some examples where two parts of nature, such as animals and plants, are working together. You can either describe or draw them as you find them.

☆ Was there anything you saw in the garden that spoiled it? What was it?

The Future

☆ The plants you see today all have finely tuned reproductive mechanisms to ensure the survival of the species into the next generation. You will almost certainly have seen the flowers, but did you see any evidence of fruit in the garden today?

☆ The idea that a person's life or work bears fruit is a familiar one. What fruit has your life borne so far?

☆ What means do we have to ensure the survival of our faith into the next generation?

75

Spiritual Notepad

It was the belief of the apostle Paul that if we would look closely at the world itself, we could find clues that point to the reality of the unseen but powerful God who is behind this visible world. He wrote, 'Since the creation of the world God's invisible qualities – his eternal power and divine nature – have been clearly seen, being understood from what has been made' (Romans 1:20).

As you look around you in the garden, see how many clues you can find that point to the power of God or indeed to any other of his characteristics. Make a note of them below.

Pause 4 Thought

The kiss of the sun for pardon,
the song of the birds for mirth,
one is nearer God's heart in a garden
than anywhere else on earth.

Dorothy Frances Gurney

Discovery

☆ Dorothy Frances Gurney, who wrote the poem on the Pause 4 Thought page, was married to a priest. After your experience today, can you see why she expressed these thoughts? Do you agree with her?

☆ As you walked around today, did you stick to the pathways, or were you tempted to wander off them? Is that typical of your personality?

☆ The story at the start of this section expressed the idea that flowers or plants can 'speak' to us and that if we are able to see that, then it can help build up our faith. Has anything you have seen today 'spoken' to you?

☆ In what ways have you been encouraged in your faith as you have visited the gardens today?

Words That Count

Then the man and his wife heard the sound of the Lord God as he was walking in the garden in the cool of the day . . .

Genesis 3:8

Spend a few moments walking quietly and reflecting on this verse.

Time 2 Talk

Choose a favourite place in the garden to quietly explore this prayer:

Father, I have been confronted again today with your creation.
Some of it is delicate and intricate,
other parts are rugged and wild.
Thank you that you have been in the garden with me,
whether I have been very aware of it or not.
Help me as I continue to think about you as the God of all creation,
and work out what that means in the way
I live my life in this world.

(You can add a few words of your own here to make this prayer personal to you.)

Amen

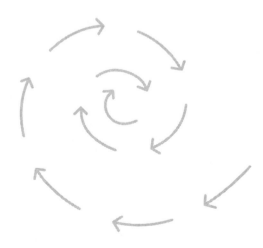

Scrapbook

☆ Stick here some leaflet, picture or other memento of your time at the gardens today.

☆ Is there anything, such as a small plant, that you can buy and take home as a reminder of your experience today?

5. At the Theme Park

A Roller Coaster Ride

Visit to:	Date:

Before You Go

Life often seems more akin to a roller coaster ride than a quiet walk beside a river!

Everybody has times when life seems to get out of control, when we can seemingly do nothing but hang on tight to whatever life will throw us, and hope that we will still be in one piece at the end of it.

But is this all there is to life, or does God intend us to have other experiences? What sort of parent is he? The one who stands over his child with a whip to make sure he does his homework, or the one who is desperate to go out and play with his kids?

Perhaps a day at the theme park will help you discover something of God's character that up to now has been hidden from view.

Walt Disney, and others like him, spent their whole lives encouraging us to have fun, but in a world cluttered with so many problems does God mind if we go out and 'play'?

Practical Preparation

☆ Choose a theme park or funfair that is likely to have a wide range of rides and experiences.

☆ Plan anything from half to a full day, depending on how many rides you want to join.

☆ The questions are based in two sections, the first section to be answered beforehand, perhaps even on the journey to the theme park, and the second set to be answered at the end of your day out.

☆ This is an ideal adventure to do with a friend, but it's up to you how many of the questions you share.

☆ Be prepared to bring back something as a reminder of your visit.

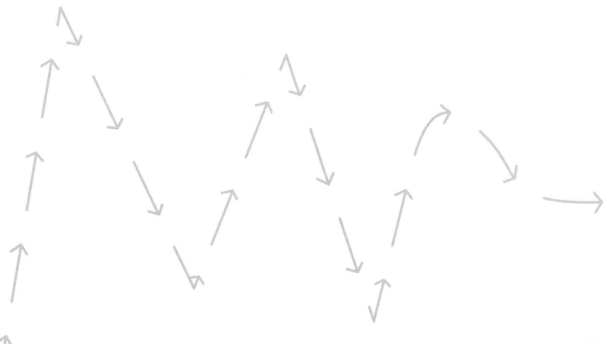

The Experience

☆ When you arrive, acclimatize yourself to the park and its attractions by having a stroll around.

☆ If you haven't already, spend time considering the first set of questions.

☆ Choose which rides you would like to go on, and those you would not.

☆ Have fun on the rides you have chosen!

☆ Look at the second set of questions.

☆ Pray that God will help you unwind and relax while having fun and learning about him.

The Adventure

Things to Think about Before You Ride

☆ When did you last have time out just for yourself?

☆ Do you find it easy taking time off for relaxation and pleasure? What made you answer this way?

☆ Do you think God ever relaxes, has fun or enjoys himself? Why and how might this be?

☆ Do you believe that God made you to have fun and to enjoy yourself? Why do you think this?

☆ Do you imagine God will accompany you on the rides?

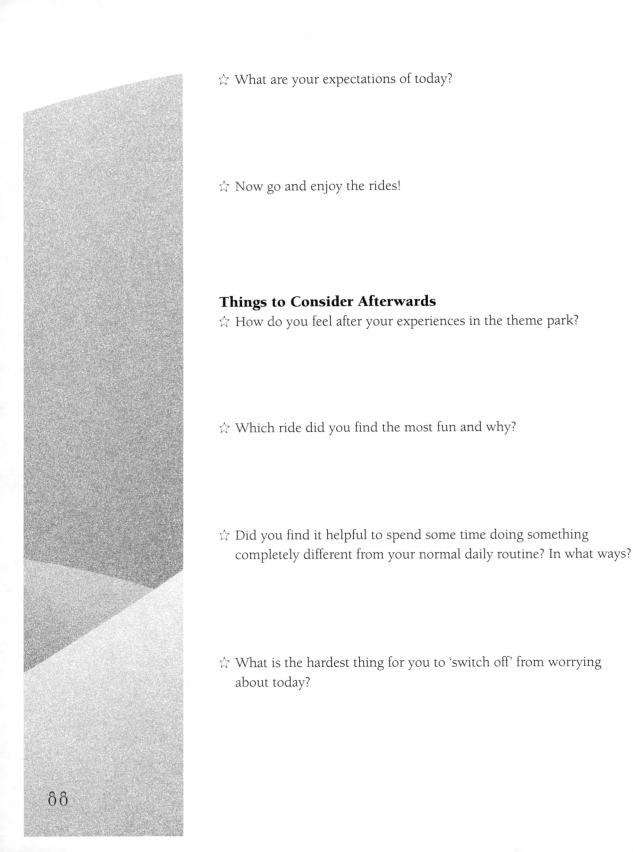

☆ What are your expectations of today?

☆ Now go and enjoy the rides!

Things to Consider Afterwards

☆ How do you feel after your experiences in the theme park?

☆ Which ride did you find the most fun and why?

☆ Did you find it helpful to spend some time doing something completely different from your normal daily routine? In what ways?

☆ What is the hardest thing for you to 'switch off' from worrying about today?

A Bumpy Ride?

☆ When on the rides, how did it feel not having complete control over where you were going?

☆ Although you had a free choice over what ride you went on, does it sometimes seem as if you have little or no choice over which of 'life's rides' you experience? How do you handle this?

☆ How much trust did you place in the rides and their operators that you would be kept from harm?

☆ What other aspects of your day brought you enjoyment?

Pause 4 Thought

Did you know that the Bible says 'Do not worry about tomorrow' in one form or another, 366 times? This is one 'Don't worry' for every day of the week and one extra for leap year!

God obviously knows that we sometimes carry far more fears than necessary and that we need to hear him telling us not to worry, each and every day of our lives!

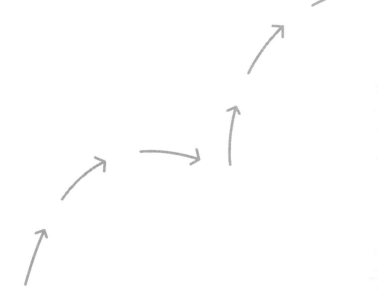

Time 2 Talk

Thank you, God, that you understand how much I worry.

Sometimes I feel bad because it seems my faith in you should stop me worrying so much. Then I end up worrying that you will be angry with me because it looks as though I don't trust you as much as I think I should!

I know deep down that worrying doesn't help, but being able to ask for your help does, and I believe that you are never too tired to listen to me.

I realize that our unique relationship works best when prayer and action work together. Please help me to do this more and more, little by little.

Amen.

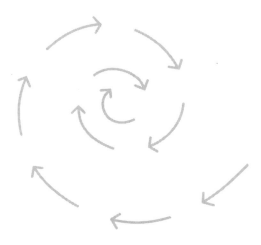

Words That Count

Can any one of you by worrying add a single hour to your life?

Matthew 6:27 TNIV

Spiritual Notepad

☆ Write or draw a description of the ride that could symbolize your experience of life at this moment and explain why.

Discovery

☆ Is there anything else that comes to mind after your day out with God at the theme park?

☆ Why not plan your own day out just to enjoy yourself? Where will you choose to go?

Scrapbook

☆ Stick a reminder here of your day at the theme park.

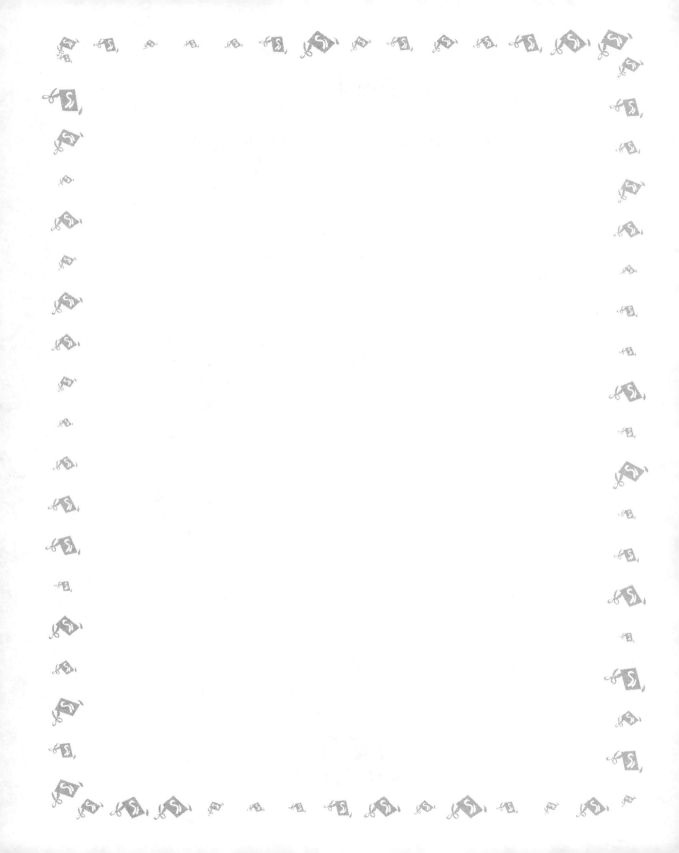

6. The Sports Game

Teamwork

Visit to:	Date:

Before You Go

A surprising number of stars in the world of sports combine their sporting ability with a living faith in God. The film *Chariots of Fire* brought the exciting story of athlete Eric Liddell to the attention of a great many people. But he is only one of many sporting heroes who have not only achieved great success in sport, but have also been public about their relationship with God. Whether in tennis or golf, soccer or athletics, cricket or basketball, some of the most successful performers make no secret of the fact that God is central to their lives, even above the passion of their game.

Perhaps one of the reasons for this is that sports men and women can see parallels between the game they play and the lives they live. As you enjoy a sports game today, see how that experience can create opportunities for you to see new things in the arena of your own life.

Practical Preparation

☆ Sports is one of our main leisure time pursuits, with many people either playing or watching a wide variety of games. This chapter is designed for both those who play and those who watch.

☆ First of all, select your sporting event. To get the best out of this chapter, it will need to be some kind of team game. It could be that you are going to play yourself, or planning to travel to see a game or you may be just watching one on television.

☆ This chapter works very well if two or three of you work on it together, where it is possible.

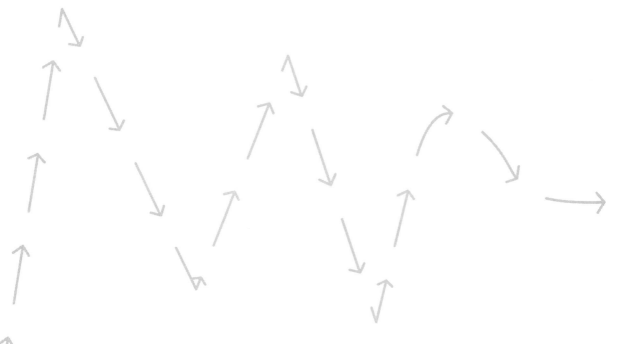

The Experience

☆ If you are watching the game on television, you may be able to answer some of the questions as the game goes along, but if you are part of a large crowd that may not be practical. And, of course, if you are playing, you won't be able to do so with your book in one hand and a pencil in the other!

☆ Whatever you decide, remember the significant parts of your experience and spend some time afterwards thinking through the issues raised.

☆ Before you experience the game, you will need to glance through this chapter first, to give you an idea of what to look for. In fact, the very first question will need to be answered even before the game begins!

The Adventure

Watching the Game

☆ Before the game starts, what do you think the result might be?

☆ As you watch, consider what you think are the best and the worst features of the game.

☆ Did you notice any examples of good or bad sportsmanship?

☆ What excites you and makes you passionate about the game?

Looking At the Players

☆ How many players were involved in the game?

☆ Can you give some examples of great individual sporting ability that you saw?

☆ Give some examples of good teamwork that you observed.

☆ How do relationships between team members make a difference to the way that the team performs?

Observing the Match Referee or Umpire

☆ Almost every game has someone who knows the rules thoroughly and who is there to ensure that they are adhered to and that any cheating or foul play is penalized. What did the referee or umpire have to do in the game you saw?

☆ Did you feel that the refereeing or umpiring was done fairly, or would you like to have seen any different decisions made?

☆ What was the hardest thing the referee or umpire had to do?

☆ What was the end result of the game, and were you right in your early predictions? Do you think this represents a true reflection of the game?

☆ If you had to give a 'player of the match' award, who would you give it to and why?

Viewing the Crowd

☆ How many people do you think were watching the game?

☆ What signs were there that the crowd got really involved in the game?

☆ Why do you think that players appreciate the support given by a good crowd?

☆ Did you observe today's crowd ever becoming hostile towards any player or referee?

☆ What do you imagine the game would have been like if there had been no spectators?

Is Life Like a Game?

☆ In what ways does your life feel like a game to you?

☆ Do you see yourself winning or losing at this stage in the game? Why is that?

☆ Who or what do you see as the 'opposition', working against you?

☆ What obstacles do you have to overcome in your game at the moment?

☆ God sees the whole of the game of your life, even the bits that are invisible to other onlookers. Which features of your game might God be commending you on today?

☆ Are there any skills in the game of your life that God might be wanting you to learn or brush up on?

☆ The aim of the game you saw today is probably self-evident. But what would you say is the aim of the game of your life?

☆ People often get very passionate about their team or their sport. What spiritual passions do you think you have?

How Is a Church Like a Team?

☆ Altogether the whole team involved in any game will comprise of more than those on the field or pitch. As well as the players, the wider team will include the spectators, the managers, the coach, the substitutes and possibly even a physiotherapist! People have likened the church to a team. If there is some truth in that comparison, what is your role in the church's team?

☆ What would you honestly say are your own strengths and weaknesses in terms of your role in the team of God's church?

☆ If your captain was to have a discussion with you about your relationships with the team, what practical steps might be offered to you to further enhance the strength of your personal teamwork?

Is There a Referee for the Game of Life?

☆ Are there people who seem to think it is their job to act as referee or umpire in the game of your life?

☆ How do you cope if their decisions and comments seem to be unfair?

☆ Every game operates with a set of rules that are there to make the game playable. They are not meant to restrict but to enable, and to make possible a game that could not happen if anyone could do whatever they felt like. What happens to us when we break the rules that God has given to us for our game of life?

☆ One of the tasks of the umpire or referee is to signal the end of the game. What are your thoughts about the final blowing of the whistle on your life?

☆ How will you know whether you have won or lost?

Pause 4 Thought

Just as players in a game are encouraged and spurred on by the crowd, so there is a crowd that encourages us as we run in the race of life.

The New Testament book of Hebrews is written to encourage Christians in their faith. In it we read that 'we are surrounded by such a huge crowd of witnesses to the life of faith' (Hebrews 12:1 NLT).

Whilst some of that crowd are people we can see here on earth, the suggestion is that there is also a great unseen crowd of witnesses in heaven.

As you think about this, ask yourself these questions:

☆ When do you feel supported by the people you know here on earth who watch you being a Christian?

☆ When do you feel intimidated by those people who are watching your Christian life?

☆ What do you find helpful about the idea that there is a crowd of spectators in heaven who are urging you on and cheering you as you take part in the game of life?

☆ Is there anyone in that crowd you can particularly imagine who is shouting your name?

☆ Thinking of those who are urging you on, what would you like them to shout to you today?

Words That Count

In the words below the author, Paul, refers to the athletic games that were commonly held in a number of larger Greek towns at that time. These games were a cut-down version of the great ancient Olympic Games held in Athens, and it is quite likely that Paul had attended such an event. If he had not actually been to the games, then he knew a lot about them, and assumed that his Greek readers would be familiar with them too.

Paul knows that in the games the main prize only goes to one contestant, but here he talks about a game in which we all can be victorious and prize-winners, provided we have the right attitude.

> Do you not know that in a race all the runners run, but only one gets the prize? Run in such a way as to get the prize. Everyone who competes in the games goes into strict training. They do it to get a crown that will not last; but we do it to get a crown that will last forever. Therefore I do not run like a man running aimlessly; I do not fight like a man beating the air. No, I beat my body and make it my slave so that after I have preached to others, I myself will not be disqualified for the prize.
>
> *1 Corinthians 9:24–27*

Spiritual Notepad

☆ We began by looking at the idea that there are parallels between a game of sport and our lives. Now would be a good time to try and summarize what these are below.

☆ In the passage on the previous page, Paul brings together a number of sporting pictures and metaphors and seems to progress from one to the other in quick succession. How many references to sporting themes can you find in the quotation above and what spiritual truths are drawn out of them for us?

Time 2 Talk

You can pray your own prayer arising out of your reflections today, or you can use words like these:

Lord, teach us how to best play this game of life that we are involved in.
Give us the encouragement that we need to keep going,
and make us aware of all those who are actively supporting us in what we do.
Help us when we feel as if our energy is running out
and we do not know how to keep going.
Show us where we need to learn new skills,
and how to improve our play.
Enable us to see ourselves as part of a team
and to enjoy sharing our game with others.
Remind us that you are the referee with the whistle,
so that we always keep our game within the guidelines you have given us.
Finally, when the game is over,
may we hear your voice saying, 'Well done'.
We ask this prayer in Jesus name.

Amen.

Discovery

☆ Write down the names of as many of those famous sports men and women who have been active Christians as you can think of. You can keep adding to this list in the future as you become aware of more names to include in it. You could then choose one or two names from the list and pray for them today, as well as remembering others on different occasions.

Scrapbook

As a record of the game you have seen, you can stick here a ticket, or some other memento of the game. Alternatively, you could cut out and stick in some newspaper cuttings about the game or else draw something that truly represented the game for you. You could even, if you wanted to, write your own match summary, as if you were a sports journalist.

7. The Restaurant

Taste and See

Visit to:	Date:

Before You Go

My father once commented how good it was of God to make food enjoyable to eat. 'We would all have wasted away if eating had been a chore,' he said. 'And what wonderful experiences we would be missing.'

Food is not just about sustenance and enjoyment, however, there are many other spiritual parallels to be had from a meal in a restaurant. Is God really to be found in such a place? It seems that the Bible is crammed full of instances when all sorts of interesting things happened over a meal, from the fruit picked and eaten by Adam and Eve in Genesis to the great banquet we all look forward to in Revelation.

Today it seems that speed and choice are the most important facets to eating out. Gone are the times when we would regularly dress up for dinner, and relax for many hours over several courses. Fast food or the temptation to look at your watch between visits from the waiter has become the norm. The world seems to turn a lot faster than ever before, and it has certainly affected our eating habits.

Stress of choice can sometimes cause us to want others to choose for us. You can't just opt for a simple mug of coffee anymore. It's Cappuccino, Americana, Espresso, Latte, or just plain filter. Then it's with extra milk or cream, with chocolate or cinnamon, with sugar or not . . . Phew!

So did Jesus enjoy a good meal? You bet. If the Pharisees had the nerve to nickname Jesus a glutton and a drunkard, it must have been because he spent so much of his time chatting to people over a meal. Perhaps this is what he wants to do today. Are you hungry?

Practical Preparation

☆ This is an ideal adventure to do with a friend, but it will still work if you decide to eat alone.

☆ You can start your adventure at any type of food outlet from an English Pub to an American Diner. A McDonald's will work just as well as a posh restaurant.

☆ If possible, try and pick somewhere you have not eaten at before.

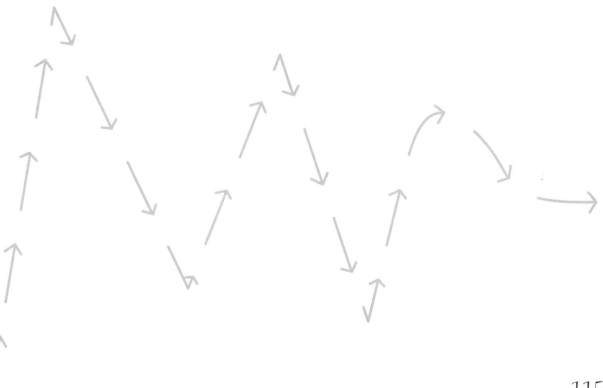

The Experience

☆ This adventure is in two halves. The first part can be done before you leave, and the second afterwards. If you have decided to have an evening meal, you could even answer the second half of the questions the following day if you prefer.

☆ Ask God to reveal himself to you during your meal and in your experience of the restaurant.

The Adventure

Working Up an Appetite

☆ What type of restaurant have you chosen?

☆ What elements have affected your choice of restaurant?

☆ What are the reasons behind your choice to dine alone or with a friend?

☆ Explain why this is to be a quick meal or one with no time limit.

☆ How wide and varied would you like the menu to be?

☆ How long do you imagine it will take you to choose from the menu?

☆ Do you know what type of food you will choose, before you even see the menu?

☆ What essentials of the meal are you looking forward to?

☆ Are you likely to say a 'grace' of any kind before your meal? Why or why not?

☆ If your meal symbolized something, what would it be?

☆ If Jesus was your special guest at the table, what do you think you would talk about?

On Reflection

☆ What did you finally choose from the menu?

☆ If you met the person who prepared your meal, what would you say to them?

☆ Was there anything in the restaurant that held a particular spiritual symbolism for you?

Choice

☆ Were there any restrictions, self imposed or otherwise, on how you chose from the menu?

☆ Did anyone else help you make your choices?

☆ Did anything else influence your choice in any way?

☆ Can you list some of the recent daily decisions you have had to make?

☆ What do you think have been the most significant choices you have ever made?

☆ How important is choice to you?

☆ Can you remember any incidents in your life that caused you to feel your choice was taken away?

☆ Do you think God cares about this?

☆ How often do you involve God in your day-to-day decisions?

☆ Can you draw some simple icons that would represent the sort of choices that you imagine God makes day by day?

Beyond the Banquet

☆ Meals often bring people together. What brings you and God together?

☆ Food brings many physical benefits, but what items would be on your spiritual menu?

☆ We like to eat different things each day, but do you think God offers a varied menu for our lives?

☆ Are you adventurous in tasting different types of food? Is your answer the same, spiritually speaking?

☆ We all dislike some food and crave other types. What spiritual food do you shy away from, and which do you never have enough of?

☆ What spiritual parallels does the following poem have for you?

> Jack Spratt would eat no fat,
> His wife would eat no lean.
> But together, sure enough
> They would lick the platter clean

☆ What do you think the following types of meals represent in spiritual terms?

Snack:

Take-away:

Family meal:

Dinner at a restaurant:

Banquet:

Scrapbook

☆ Either stick a copy of the menu or your bill here.

Spiritual Notepad

☆ What biblical meals can you recall, and what do they say to you?

Pause 4 Thought

Right from the start of creation, God gave us the ability to choose. God's first decision in Genesis was to create the heavens and the earth. Adam and Eve's first choice was to do it their way. Despite God's decision to allow Adam and Eve the free will to do this, he also decided to follow them out of the Garden and into their everyday lives.

Perhaps our biggest daily choice is how much we allow God in.

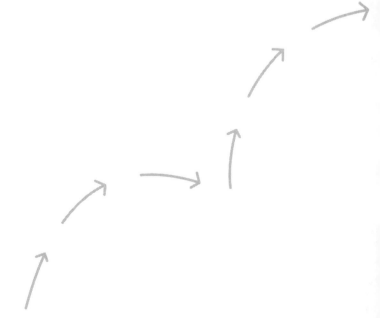

Time 2 Talk

Sometimes I stand before you, Lord,
Tired, dirty, and uncertain whether you still love me.
I've made so many wrong decisions,
Taken all the wrong turnings,
Made deliberate detours,
Yet in amazement I know
That the door is still open and your feast awaits.

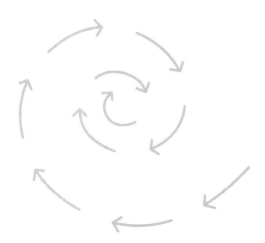

Words That Count

I chose you and appointed you so that you might go and bear fruit –
fruit that will last.

John 15:16 TNIV

Discovery

☆ What aspects of God did you notice at the restaurant today?

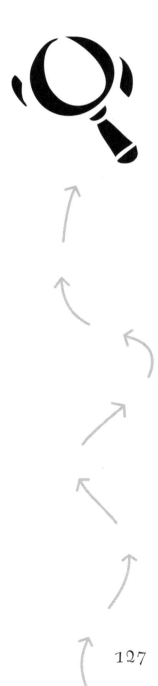

8. In the Shopping Mall

Life's Essentials

Visit to:	Date:

Before You Go

Did you know that there is a book in the Bible that does not mention the name of God, not even once? Neither does it mention Jesus or the Spirit. So you might conclude that in this book God is not really there. But that would be a complete misunderstanding of the story of Esther. For, in fact, God is there even when he is not spoken of. It is as if he is hiding in the wings and directing operations from off-stage.

The story of Esther has many twists and turns in it. (If you are not familiar with it, I think you'll find it to be a good read.) It all begins with a queen refusing to do what the king commanded her to do, and as a consequence losing her place in the royal household. Disaster? Perhaps, but God was at work in this. Next, when the king decides to hold a beauty competition to find himself a new wife, God saw to it that the right person won. It wasn't evident at the time, but later on it was crucial. And even in a moment when the king cannot sleep and decides to have a read in the middle of the night, God organizes everything to make sure that when he does some reading, it triggers a memory of something he had intended to do.

So when things look all set for disaster, God is quietly active and suddenly the narrative takes a turn in a new and better direction. Therefore, although God does not have his name written on every page, and indeed not on any page, this is still his story and he is the director of the plot and brings the story to a satisfying end. His name may not be visible, but his presence is there.

Now do you think that you can find God in a mall full of shops? Some people might say that it is impossible. After all, it has been suggested that shopping today is becoming a substitute religion, because people prefer to turn to 'retail therapy' rather than to religious faith! So if, as some people say, shops are centres of consumerism or materialism, dedicated to the gods of choice and places where multinational corporations are all powerful, then can we go there to find God? Is it possible that shopping and spirituality could go hand in hand? Well, you are about to see if you can look at all this in a new light.

God's name may not be lit up in coloured lights, but perhaps you'll find that, as you scratch beneath the surface, God is as much there as he is anywhere else.

So that's your journey of discovery!

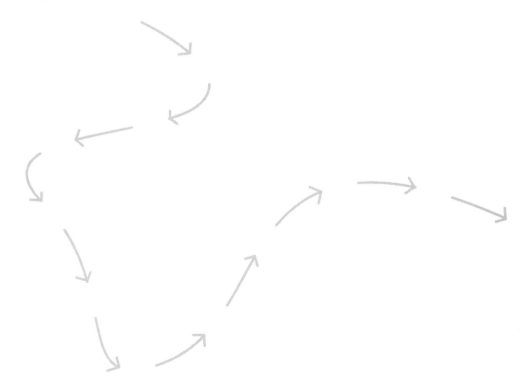

Practical Preparation

☆ For this activity you will need to find a place with a reasonable number of shops.

☆ Allow yourself time to window-shop, to explore and to think, as well as possibly to buy something.

☆ If you are not able to get out, you might find that some of the sections could be done with some home shopping catalogues in front of you, or through shopping on the Internet.

☆ A thought: While you are at the shops why not buy a small present as a token of appreciation for someone? Perhaps you could make it a gift for someone you do not normally give presents to!

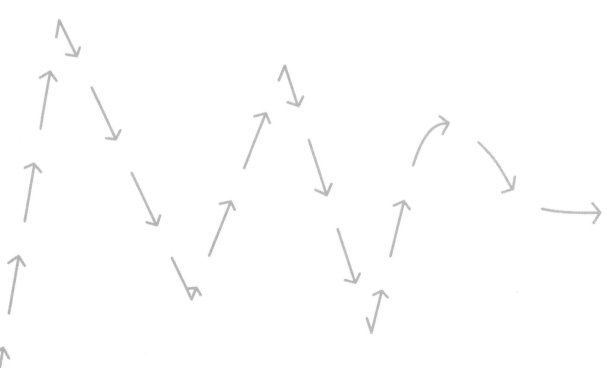

The Experience

☆ Either before you head out for the shops or when you arrive, have a quick look through this chapter so as to give you an idea of what you will be looking for.

☆ The various sections are best filled in as you go around, and this means that you have to jump around a bit from one section to another as you explore the various shops.

☆ You can fill in your book after you have left the store if you feel awkward about doing so while you are actually inside.

The Adventure

One World

'No man is an island,' wrote poet John Donne, coining a famous phrase. Today we are more aware than ever that we live in one world with all its interdependence, its links and its connections. As you shop you will inevitably find goods from all over this world and from all kinds of different places.

☆ As you go along, make a note of some of the more interesting products you find, coming from various parts of the world.

☆ Did you make any discoveries doing this?

☆ Do you ever wonder about people in other places who make what we buy? Should they be a concern of ours, just because they have produced our goods?

☆ What might you feel or say if you met them face to face?

Body, Intellect, Feelings, Spirit

☆ Although as human beings we are an integrated whole, there are various strands that make us the people we are. These include our body, our intellect, our feelings and our spirit. As you wander through the shops, look for products that provide for these different parts of our humanity.

Products made for my body:

    Product

    Shop

Products made for my intellect:

    Product

    Shop

Products made for my feelings:

    Product

    Shop

Products made for my spirit:

    Product

    Shop

☆ Is any part of me over-provided for by these shops?

☆ What part of me is least catered for in these shops?

Work and Leisure

☆ Both work and leisure are gifts to us and essential parts of being alive. After all, very early on in the Bible, we discover that God can both work and rest. So have a look and see what you can notice about the gifts of work and of leisure as you wander through different shops. As you go, watch the various people who are working in the shops and the people who are there in their leisure time to browse or buy. What have you noticed about the gift of work?

☆ What have you noticed about the gift of leisure?

☆ How important is shopping to you? Does it have any hold on you? Are you alright with that?

☆ Does 'retail therapy' work for you? Why is that?

☆ How well do you balance work and leisure in your life?

What If?

☆ One of the most familiar of Rudyard Kipling's poems is simply called 'if'. It is an invitation to dream, to wonder and to imagine what might be. Here is your chance to use your imagination, as you think, *What if . . . ?* So, *if* you had to work in one of the shops that you have visited, which one would you want to work in and why?

☆ *If* you really wanted to make the world a tiny bit better, is there anything you could have spent your money on today that would do that?

☆ Jesus sometimes made some very profound pronouncements in public places. *If* Jesus was in the shops today, what do you imagine he might have said? (You can either put your own words together here or use words that you know Jesus actually said in his lifetime.)

☆ *If* you had to choose something from your shopping experience to say thank you for, what would it be?

137

Spiritual Notepad

☆ Goodness and evil surround us as two opposing spiritual realities in our world. As you look at a slice of life in the shops you visit, you should be able to see evidence of both. Have a look both at the people in the shopping mall and the commercial systems that make it what it is. You may need to look just below the surface to find evidence that points to the existence of goodness and kindness, or exploitation and oppression.

Pause 4 Thought

It is most probable that Jesus would have shopped during his lifetime, even though it wouldn't have been quite the same as your experience today. Indeed on one occasion he encountered people buying and selling in such a way that it made him really angry. He was so cross in fact that he overturned the simple counters of the merchants and tipped their goods and cash all over the floor. That must have caused pandemonium. It makes you wonder if Jesus would ever like to repeat that act anywhere else!

☆ Do you think Jesus would have been angry in the shops you visited today?

☆ Was there anything that made you angry?

☆ In one of the great stories Jesus told, he talked about people who traded with their money, did well and made a profit. They were rewarded with the words, 'Well done, good and faithful servant.' Do you think that Jesus might have given such a commendation to anyone you saw?

☆ Did anything you experienced today make you particularly happy?

Discovery

☆ If you have any reflections on your experience today you have not
  yet recorded, then note them here.

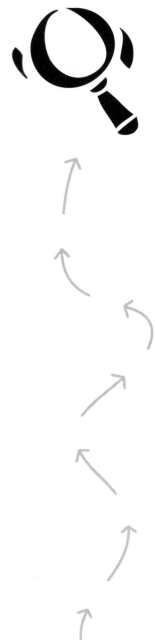

Words That Count

God . . . richly provides us with everything for our enjoyment.

1 Timothy 6:17

Time 2 Talk

There is a prayer called 'A General Thanksgiving', which is used by many churches and it has these words:

> We bless you for our creation, preservation and all the blessings of this life
>
> Give us, we pray, such a sense of your mercies that our hearts may be unfeignedly thankful
>
> and that we show forth your praise not only with our lips but in our lives.

As you read these words try and get a feeling for the prayer, and then continue it with words of your own, spoken quietly.

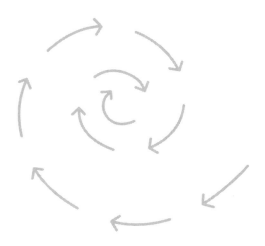

Scrapbook

☆ Try and find something that will remind you of your visit today. It may be something you have bought, a store guide, a map, a photograph or even simply a receipt for something you purchased.

☆ Don't forget to buy a small present as a token of appreciation for someone!

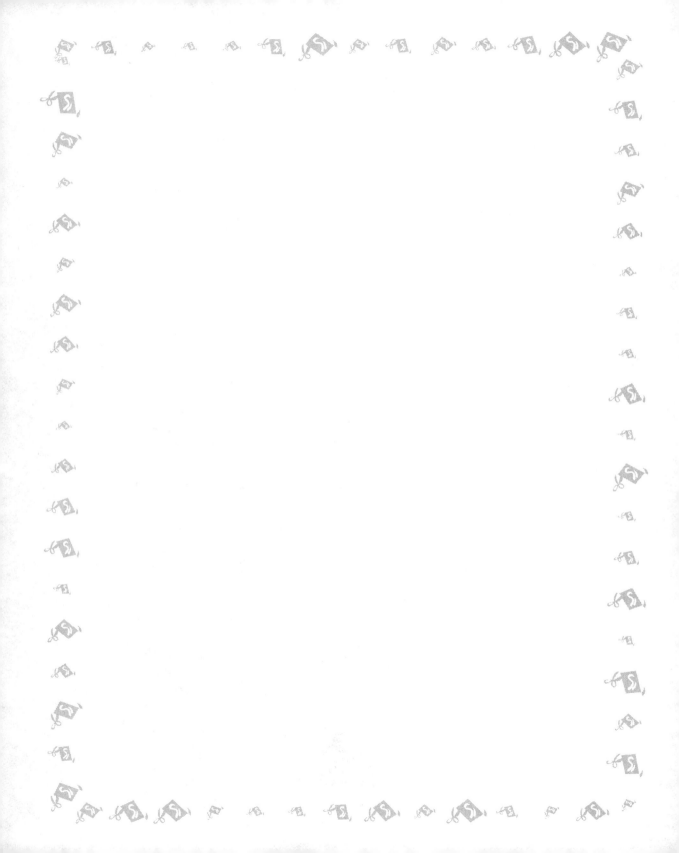

9. In the Library

Life in Print

Visit to:	Date:

Before You Go

I have no idea how many words I am exposed to each day, whether in print or through sound waves. Many of them make that proverbial journey, going in one ear and out of the other. But others stick and lodge somewhere inside me. Some will even help to shape my life through decisions I make, and things I choose to do or decide to avoid.

One of the great and influential thinkers in the early centuries of the Christian Church was a man called Augustine – a bishop from North Africa. He had a long and tortuous journey to faith with many blind alleys and detours. However, while he was agonizing over what to believe and how to live, he overheard some words being chanted by the children next door, as they played some sort of game. The words that he heard, over and over again, were these: 'Take up and read.' Suddenly they struck Augustine in a new way, as if God was saying something to him through the simple words of children playing next door. He decided to test this out and so went to his Bible, and started reading from the place he had reached previously. Once again the simple words of the Gospel seemed to speak to him personally with amazing clarity. Just one sentence from the book of Romans was enough to bring him to a place where he was certain of his faith, and to blow away all those doubts he had been struggling with for so long. The rest, as they say, is history.

As you go to the library today, you will be confronted with words of all kinds of size, colour and meaning. And God uses words like these to shape, challenge and change our lives.

Practical Preparation

☆ Choose a library to visit, if possible finding one that you have not been to before.

☆ Plan to be there for about two hours – although some people may want less time than that, and others may want more.

☆ If, for any reason, you can't get to a library, then you could try doing this activity in a large book shop, or even by browsing through an online bookstore. For example, you could try www.amazon.com.

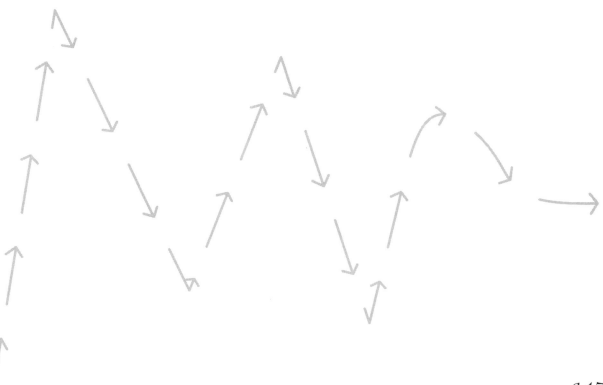

The Experience

☆ When you arrive, first get a feel for the general layout of the library and find out where the different types of books are. For this activity we recommend that you locate the following sections: (1) biography and autobiography, (2) history, (3) fiction and (4) poetry.

☆ If you prefer, you can choose two or three of these categories and just work on those, rather than trying to do all four.

☆ Once again, try to find some memento of the library that you can fix into your book at the end of the section.

☆ Begin by looking at books in the sections you have chosen. Once you have filled in all your answers, find somewhere to go either to think through your findings alone, or talk about them with a friend.

The Adventure

People with a Story to Tell: Biography and Autobiography

☆ Wander for a time among the biographical section, looking at those books that tell the story of people's lives. Pick up books that interest you and flick through them, perhaps reading a bit of the preface, the foreword or the summary on the cover.

☆ Out of all those you have seen, select one life story that really makes an impression on you, and think about it.

☆ Jesus told his followers to go out and be lights in a dark world. See if you can find life stories where God is an important factor, or where the influence of faith is clearly evident.

☆ If you wrote your own autobiography today, what might you call the book?

Stories from the Past: History

☆ Next, wander around the various history sections of the library, and see what is there. Choose two different historical periods that appeal to you in some way, and select a book from each period that you think you might enjoy.

☆ What do your choices tell you about the kind of history that inspires you?

☆ Much of the Bible is a kind of history. In the Old Testament we find the story of the birth of a nation that comes to be known as Israel. In the New Testament we encounter the history of the life and times of Jesus, and an account of the growth of the young church. What bits of biblical history do you find the most interesting?

☆ Can you work out why that is?

Stories from the Imagination: Fiction

☆ It is time to move on to discover the sections of the library that deal with fiction. You will find the books categorized into different sections. Take time to wander and look at what is there.

☆ As you walk among the books, cast your eye over the titles in front of you. Which title sounds the most exciting, or which would you most like to read?

☆ What does this title tell you about what interests you or captures your imagination?

☆ It may well be that some of the books you have encountered seem to be at odds with Christian standards or values. Ask yourself where God is in relation to this and take time to consider what God may be thinking about it all.

Power of a Poem: Poetry

☆ Some people enjoy poetry, while others claim that it does nothing for them. Whatever your views are, take the opportunity to look at some poetry today. You may find it in the Literature section and you could even have a look at some of the poetry in the children's area.

☆ Now choose one poetry book to look at, and find in it one poem that you like.

☆ The Bible contains a fair bit of poetry, especially in the book of Psalms. Go to the section marked 'Religion' and find yourself a Bible. See if you can find any poetry in it that excites you or makes you think.

☆ If you are unsure what bits of poetry to read in the Bible, look up some of these ideas:

The Psalms
Proverbs 8
Isaiah 9:2–7, 11:2–9
Jeremiah 8:18–22
Lamentations 3:22–42
Joel 2:1–9
Micah 4:1–4
Philippians 2:5–11

Spiritual Notepad

☆ You can discover a lot in the library, about others and even about yourself. Either choose one of the book titles that you have listed above, or another book you have come across, to find a book title that best describes your life at the moment.

☆ How might you talk to God about the book title you have just selected?

☆ How do you imagine God might reply to what you have said?

☆ Did you notice any recurring theme in the books you selected today?

Pause 4 Thought

Most people, at some time in their lives, need to have an X-ray. This wonderful invention enables us to see inside our bodies and to observe problems that are not visible externally. The doctor is there to help us interpret our X-ray pictures and to show us what we ought to do about them. Your visit to the library today may well have enabled you to get a glimpse of what is going on inside your life at the moment.

Discovery

☆ What are the most significant discoveries you have made about yourself, or what ideas have come to you in your visit to the library today?

Words That Count

O Lord, you have searched me
and you know me.
You know when I sit and when I rise;
you perceive my thoughts from afar.
You discern my going out and my lying down;
you are familiar with all my ways.
Before a word is on my tongue
you know it completely, O Lord.

Psalm 139:1–4

Time 2 Talk

Remembering that one day Jesus likened himself to a doctor, why not share your thoughts with God? You could also ask him to show you what to do with them.

Here is a prayer you could use:

> *Father, whatever I may discover about myself is not news to you, as you know me better than I know myself. Sometimes I am preoccupied with things that I cannot seem to sort out, or I find myself overwhelmed by things outside my control. Thank you that you are always there with me and that, whatever is going on in my life today, you are there to help me be strong and to move forwards. May I find support and encouragement from your presence with me today.*
>
> *Amen.*

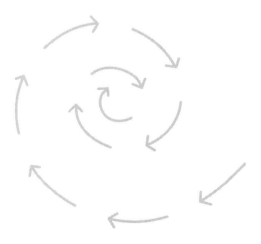

Scrapbook

☆ Stick here some memento of your visit to the library.

10. At the Cemetery

My Eternity

Visit to:	Date:

Before You Go

Although the world is made up of people from every walk of life, colour and nation, there is one thing that every single person, whether king or pauper, is guaranteed to experience: death.

Life and death go hand in hand, but very often we avoid morbid subjects as much as possible. Perhaps we are afraid of bringing old feelings to the surface, but in fact, this is probably the best way to deal with them.

But is it really possible to find God in a cemetery? Consider the following story.

One little boy was wandering home from Sunday school and dawdling along the way. He scuffed his shoes in the grass. He found a caterpillar. He found a fluffy dandelion and blew out all of its seeds. A bird's nest in the tree above him was another wonder that caught his eager eyes.

A neighbour watched his zigzag course and called to him from his front lawn. He asked the boy where he'd been, and what he was doing.

'I've been to Sunday school,' said the boy. Turning over a piece of soil, he picked up a wiggly worm, saying, 'I've learned a lot about God.'

'Hmm . . . a very fine way for a boy to spend his time,' the neighbour replied. 'If you can tell me where God is, I'll give you some extra pocket money.'

Quick as a flash, the boy's answer came, nor were his words faint, 'I'll give you some pocket money, Mister, if you can tell me where God ain't.'

Practical Preparation

☆ Choose a cemetery that is not too large. You need to be able to walk around it within half an hour or so. If you can't get to one, take a virtual tour. We suggest highgate-cemetery.org/index.asp or www.interment.net/Default.htm.

☆ Pray that God will speak to you as you start your journey.

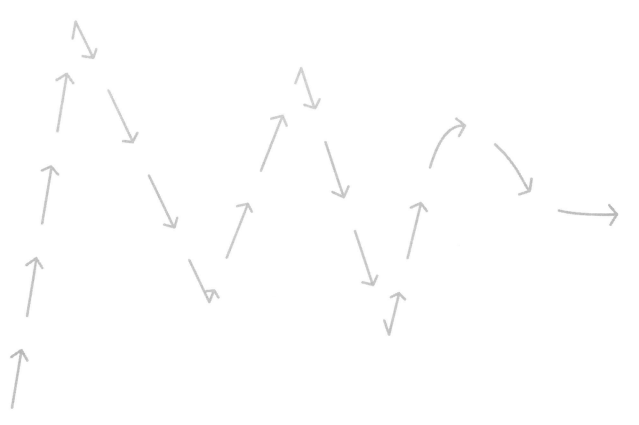

The Experience

☆ Plan about two hours for your visit.

☆ The questions can be answered as you walk around, looking at the gravestones.

☆ Leave some time at the end of your discovery to sit down for some refreshment and to reflect on your answers.

☆ This is a good adventure to do by yourself, but if you are doing this with a friend, arrange a time to meet up at the end to compare notes.

The Adventure

☆ Note down the inscription of a tombstone that

Encourages you:

Causes you to feel sad:

Makes you smile:

Intrigues you the most:

Gives unusual details about that person's life:

☆ Can you find the gravestone of the person who lived the longest?

☆ Which was the shortest life you came across?

☆ Have you found a stone that reflects your own life at this moment in time? What words do you relate to personally?

Pause 4 Thought

The Ship

What is dying?
I am standing upon the seashore.
  A ship at my side spreads her sails to the morning breeze
  and starts for the blue ocean.
  She is an object of beauty and strength and I stand and watch her
until at length she hangs like a speck of white cloud
just where the sea and sky come down to mingle with each other.
Then someone at my side says:
  'There! She's gone.'
Gone where! Gone from my sight – that is all.
She is just as large in mast and hull and spar as she was
  when she left my side,
and just as able to bear her load of living freight
  to the place of destination.
Her diminished size is in me, not in her;
and just at the moment when someone at my side says,
'There! She's gone,'
there are other eyes watching her coming,
  and other voices ready to take up the glad shout,
  'There she comes!'
And that is dying.

Henry Van Dyke

Take a moment out to reflect on the following:

☆ Do you ever wonder how long you will live? If you were to take a guess, how old would you be and why?

☆ How much do you imagine that the length of your life is in your own hands?

☆ Do you think that all the people buried here had completed their life's journey according to their wishes?

☆ If there is a church building nearby, do you feel it has any symbolic relationship to those buried here?

☆ What is your view of death? Are you frightened of the subject and if so, why?

☆ If God was in this cemetery, where do you think you would find him?

☆ Do any words of scripture spring to mind at this moment? If so, perhaps you would like to write them here in your own words.

Scrapbook

☆ If you were to write your own inscription or epitaph, what would
it say?

Spiritual Notepad

☆ Looking back at the gravestones, jot down any inscriptions that
  have a spiritual feel to them, (a verse, a poem, a symbol for
  example) and put an asterisk against those you relate to personally.

Time 2 Talk

☆ Pick one of the verses or inscriptions you have chosen, and turn it into a prayer for your life today. You can write it here in your own words if you wish.

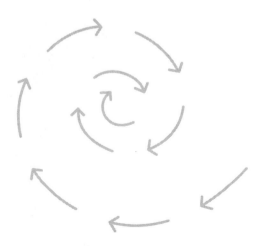

Words That Count

For You, O Lord, have delivered my soul from death,
my eyes from tears,
my feet from stumbling,
that I may walk before the Lord
in the land of the living.

Psalms 116:8

Discovery

☆ What aspects of life and death have you been reminded of today?

☆ What aspects of God did you discover at the cemetery today?

☆ How do you feel after your visit to the cemetery?

☆ Has your view of God changed in any way today?

11. By the Riverside

A Never-Ending Stream

Visit to:	Date:

Before You Go

We all need to escape from time to time. A show business friend of mine is a pilot and has his own aeroplane. He loves nothing better than to literally rise above all the stress and pressure of daily life. Up in the clouds he gets a God's eye view of the world, and things that seemed so big and imposing before are suddenly shrunk down to size. Once he sees how the land lies, and how things begin to take on perspective, he can start to relax.

When I asked to take a look at the engine of his biplane, I was astonished. 'That engine is no bigger than my lawnmower!' I exclaimed. 'How on earth does it get you up so high?' It turns out that one little spark plug can create enough energy to turn the rotor blades and get his craft soaring high in the sky and away from it all.

It struck me that if it only took something so small to help remove him from the tension of everyday life, then it must be possible for me too.

My way of escape is by the river, and a simple walk beside it can help turn off all the anxieties I have collected over the last few days. It also creates space for me to think and, away from the general clamour of life, allows my mind to wander in any direction it needs to. Despite the sometimes rushing activity of the water, calmness and tranquillity seem to descend on me, and the cares of the world around soon melt away.

I prefer rivers to lakes because a flowing stream seems more alive and less liable to stagnate. The life contained in, on and around a river is always abundant, no matter how deep or how wide. There is always something to see, something new to discover, as you are about to find out.

Practical Preparation

☆ Choose a river to visit that is not too far away. It doesn't matter if you have been there many times before as you will be looking at it from a whole new angle today.

☆ If you like, bring a camera to take photos of your river that you can place in your scrapbook later.

    If you can't get to a river, try using pictures of rivers in a book or website. We suggest www.livingrivers.org or www.ukrivers.net.

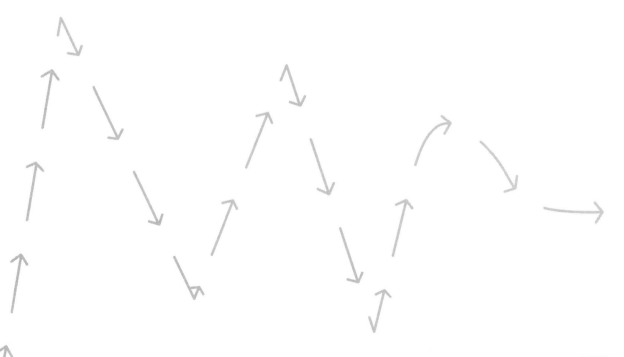

☆ You could take some nibbles, a picnic or a drink with you.

☆ This is an ideal day to do alone.

☆ Pray that God will open your mind as you walk and think and talk to him.

The Experience

☆ Plan two hours to combine walking, sitting and contemplating your discovery.

☆ As you enjoy your walk of tranquillity, perhaps you would like to stop every now and again to answer the questions. Alternatively, you can read and write, as you walk, but just make sure you don't fall in the river!

☆ The questions are set in four sections, so it's best to answer them in order.

☆ As well as looking at the whole picture, take a closer look at the smaller details too.

The Adventure

Your River

☆ How do you imagine your river came into being?

☆ Take a closer look at one particular part of your river. What do you observe?

☆ How deep is the river?

☆ Does it look as though it might run dry, or is it flowing well?

☆ How does this relate to your spiritual life at the moment?

☆ How fast is the river flowing?

☆ Can you keep up with it?

☆ Does this relate to the speed of your own life at the moment?

☆ Are there any obstacles in its way?

☆ How does your river deal with obstacles?

☆ Is there a song or tune that springs to mind when thinking about your river, or being out of doors?

Life in Abundance

☆ What plants or wildlife depend directly on the river?

☆ What things is your life dependent on?

☆ What is the season in which you are visiting?

☆ What differences would you expect to see during the other three seasons?

☆ What 'seasons' do you think your own life is in at the moment?

☆ What aspects of your life keep flowing like a river through all the various seasons?

How the River Flows

☆ Are you aware of the source of the river?

☆ Do you know where the river flows to?

☆ Do you know how long the river is?

☆ Can you tell how deep the river is?

☆ How clean is the river?

☆ Does your river run straight?

Spiritual Streams

☆ Which of the above questions raise parallel thoughts and questions about the course of your own life?

☆ Does any biblical verse or poem come to mind as you look at your river?

☆ Did you know that the book of Revelation says there will be no sea in heaven, but there will be the River of Life? What does this suggest to you?

Spiritual Notepad

☆ Draw a sketch to show how your own 'river of life' flows today. Perhaps include the obstacles that might be preventing it from flowing as freely as it could.

Pause 4 Thought

I watch them drift
The old familiar faces
Who fished and rode with me
By stream and wold
I watch them drift
The youthful aspirations
Shores, landmarks, beacons
Drift alike
I watch them drift
The poets and the statesman
The very streams run upward from the sea
Yet overhead the boundless arch of heaven
Still fades to night
Still blazes into day
Ah, God!
My God!
Thou wilt not drift away.

Charles Kingsley

Words That Count

But blessed is the man who trusts in the Lord,
whose confidence is in him.
He will be like a tree planted by the water
that sends out its roots by the stream.
It does not fear when heat comes;
its leaves are always green.
It has no worries in a year of drought
and never fails to bear fruit.

Jeremiah 17:7–8

Time 2 Talk

☆ Imagine God is walking beside you now, and you were talking to him. What would you say to him?

☆ What do you think he would say to you?

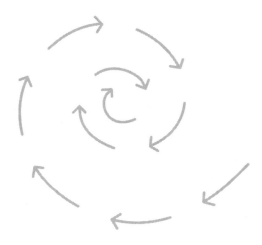

Discovery

☆ Write down what thoughts, feelings or decisions that today's day
   out has brought to the surface.

Scrapbook

☆ Be creative as you draw or stick something here as a reminder of
  your day with God by the river.

12. A Retreat

Hearing the Whispers

Visit to:	Date:

Before You Go

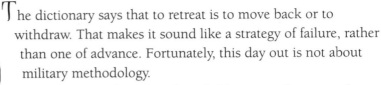

The dictionary says that to retreat is to move back or to withdraw. That makes it sound like a strategy of failure, rather than one of advance. Fortunately, this day out is not about military methodology.

I grew up at the time when children were free to go down to the park and be on their own, without the concerns of safety and protection we have today. I usually went to the park with friends, but there was one little bit of the park that I claimed for my own. There was what I called a secret pathway to it – although I'm sure others also used it. But at the end of this rather overgrown track was a seat – and I thought of it as my seat! I could sit there with no one to disturb me, for I believed that nobody knew exactly where I was. I could sit there and think, and sort out my life. And that is just what I did.

I had actually discovered the reality of retreat, without knowing it! You may already have places you go to, or times when you shut the door so that you can be alone, with space to think or to listen. Surprisingly, when we learn to retreat then we will be more equipped to advance than we ever were before!

So this exercise is about being alone, being quiet and still and being able to hear the whispers of heaven, instead of the loud and strident voices that usually occupy our ears. The secret is in learning how not to rush and in taking time to listen and think before putting pen to paper.

Practical Preparation

☆ For this adventure you will need to find somewhere to go, away from home if at all possible. In your house you are surrounded by so many distractions of things to do and problems to sort out. You need to get away from all as far as you are able.

☆ Allow yourself anything from a good hour to a whole day once you get to your place of retreat.

☆ Where you go, however, is very much up to you. If the weather is favourable, you can go somewhere outside, if possible away from the roar of traffic and noise. You may know a park or some countryside where there is a place you could sit, relax and tune in to the quietness. Others would prefer to sit in a place like a church, soaking up its atmosphere and character. Most people will want to sit down for at least some of this time, even if your retreat includes a long walk. You can decide where to go according to your circumstances, opportunities and personal taste.

☆ If you have been enjoying this book with a friend, we do want to advise you that you will not get the best out of a retreat if you try and do it together. What does work well, however, is the sharing of your experiences and ideas with someone else afterwards. So why not arrange to meet up and share with someone who has been on the same day out, talking about what you have done and thought?

☆ You will probably want to take a Bible with you.

☆ The retreat adventure will specifically ask you to have something available to eat. It doesn't matter whether this is a savoury snack, your favourite chocolate bar or a full picnic lunch, so long as you can eat it! You might also like to take a drink with you.

☆ Before you get there, however, you will need to do some very important preparation. The theme of our retreat is to be 'doors'. To prepare for this you will need to look at a number of different doors and, if at all possible, make some sketches of them on the next page, Scrapbook A. You can do as many drawings as you like and the greater the variety the better it will be. The sketches can be very simple, although it would be good to include accessories like door furniture. Start with the door to your own home, and then see how many different kinds of doors you can find as you travel to the retreat. Please give each of your drawings a number. You will not be able to share in the retreat fully until you have done this.

The Scrapbook B page will be used once you are on your retreat.

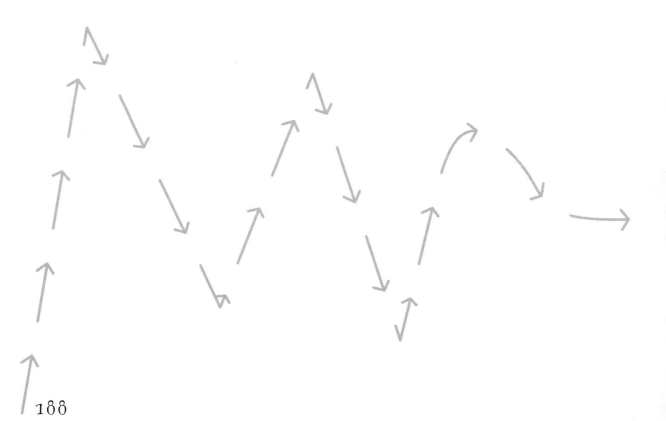

Scrapbook A

☆ Sketch in here a number of different doors, giving each door a
number.

Scrapbook B

☆ This page is for use later on in your adventure.

The Experience

☆ Once you have sketched your doors, make your way to your chosen place of retreat.

☆ As you approach your location, try to feel comfortable and relaxed. You are going to participate in the stillness around you, and you need time to let it become your friend.

☆ Don't be surprised if it takes you time to get used to the silence. It may seem strange at first and you may find that you are not very good at relaxing, but slowly you will get used to it and hopefully begin to like it.

☆ One way to help you to acclimatize to the quietness and tune into God's wavelength is by thinking about words from the Bible, and then letting those thoughts turn into prayers. The next page will give you some suggestions you can make use of.

Words That Count

☆ Pick a favourite verse, or select one of the following:

Be still, and know that I am God.

Psalm 46:10

Search me, O God, and know my heart; test me and know my anxious thoughts.

Psalm 139:23

After the wind, there was an earthquake . . . After the earthquake came a fire . . . And after the fire came a gentle whisper.

1 Kings 19:11–12

In quietness and trust is your strength.

Isaiah 30:15

'Not by might nor by power, but by my Spirit,' says the Lord Almighty.

Zechariah 4:6

Peace I leave with you; my peace I give to you.

John 14:27

☆ If you prefer to use another verse that is significant to you, write it down here.

☆ Now let your chosen words lodge in your mind by saying them several times, and even speaking them out loud if you can. Breathe them into yourself, as if they were invigorating fresh air.

Time 2 Talk

You can either use your own words to pray, or you can use the prayer below.

Pray slowly, aloud if you can, thinking about what each word means as you say it. Remember you are no longer in a hurry!

Dear God,
Help me as I leave a world that is loud, noisy and demanding,
and find a space of stillness and quiet.
May I be able to hear the whisper of your voice
and to find renewal for my life and my relationships.
May I discover more about who I am, where I am going,
and the way to get there.
Let today be a healing, encouraging and empowering time for me.
This prayer I ask through the love of God,
                                                    Amen.

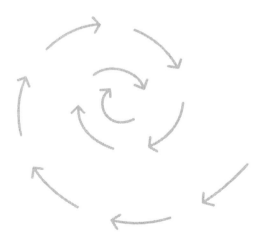

The Adventure

☆ Although you might choose to do much of your thinking as you walk, at this point you will need to find somewhere quiet to sit down.

☆ First of all take a good long hard look at the doors you have found and sketched, and note their similarities and different features.

☆ Next, try and think of other sorts of doors that you have not found. Scrapbook B has been kept for you to sketch a number of other doors, ranging from the flimsiest curtain partition to the most heavily fortified door you can imagine. Once again number your drawings, continuing on from the numbers you used on the page before.

The Door of Your Life

☆ The Bible paints a picture for us of Jesus standing outside a person's life, knocking on their door to try and gain entry. The words, 'Here I am! I stand at the door and knock' (Revelation 3:20) were the inspiration for a painting by Holman Hunt, which famously pictured Jesus, holding a lantern, knocking on an old wooden door. Which, out of all the doors you have drawn, is most like the door to your life today?

☆ What are the features of this door that match your life now?

☆ How long has the door to your life been like that?

☆ What does God think of the door he finds?

☆ If your door used to be different, which door did it most resemble at one time?

☆ If you want your door to be different in the future, what sort of door would you like to have?

☆ When do you think you might start to make changes to your door?

☆ Now take some time to think of why people knock at your door. Think of as many reasons as you can, both good and bad.

☆ Think about why God wants to knock on the door to your life. Go through the reasons you noted for people knocking on your door and tick those that apply to God knocking on the door of a person's life.

☆ Does God have any other reason for knocking on your door?

☆ How do you think God feels about the reception he is getting?

☆ God wants to come in and share a meal with the one whose door he has been knocking on. So now get out the food you have brought and use the experience of eating it as a way of inviting God into your life again as a friend you can share everything with.

Doors of Opportunity

☆ The Bible tells us about a God who opens doors of opportunity (see 2 Corinthians 2:12). People often use language like that, saying that doors have opened for them – or even that doors have closed – when referring to the opportunities they have or do not have.

☆ So now spend some time thinking about the opportunities you have in your life at this moment, and note them.

☆ Are there any doors that are shut for you at the moment? If so, can you understand in any way why that might be?

☆ If it was possible to ask for just one closed door to be opened for you today, which one would it be?

☆ How would you cope if you were told that this door had to remain closed?

☆ What do you feel about God when he does not open all the doors you want him to?

☆ What would it be like if God opened every door that you asked him to open and answered every prayer positively?

☆ Which of the pictures you have previously drawn best describes the closed doors you have been thinking of? Can you express why that is?

☆ Maybe it is time to go and have a walk and tell *God* about these pictures and what they say. But also take time to listen and look for his presence, whether you feel joyful or disappointed.

The Doors of Heaven

☆ For some reason the doors of heaven are seen as large 'pearly gates', and numerous jokes have been cracked about Peter standing there and interrogating those who want to enter. Can you remember a joke like that? If you can, then tell it to yourself and have a chuckle about it!

☆ Is there one of your Scrapbook pictures that seems to you something like the doors of heaven?

☆ If you have referred to a door, why have you chosen that one? If you have not, then what do you imagine the doors of heaven to look like?

☆ As you think about this, what does the word *heaven* mean to you?

☆ Can you remember a time when you felt as if you were knocking on heaven's door? When was that?

☆ Why were you knocking on heaven's door?

☆ Is it a bit too pushy of us to presume that we can knock on God's door for anything?

☆ What response do you seem to get when you knock?

☆ Have you ever had a different response?

☆ What do you think God feels about you knocking on his door?

☆ How much do we have to push on God's doors before they open?

Pause 4 Thought

In the account of the baptism of Jesus in the Bible, we read these words: 'And as he was praying, heaven was opened and the Holy Spirit descended on him' (Luke 3:21–22).

So the doors of heaven can and do open! This, of course, is not the only time that it has happened, and different people have experienced the opening of heaven's doors in various ways at different times.

Why did they open for Jesus at that time? Was it because of his obedience as he made himself vulnerable, standing in a queue of people, waiting to be immersed in water? Or was it his absolute commitment to God? Maybe it was his determination to be the person God wanted him to be, or perhaps it was an answer to lots of prayer. The Bible does not tell us why, but that need not stop us from trying to find answers to the question.

The truth is that God can open heaven to us so that he feels incredibly near and close. Maybe that process has just started with you on today's retreat. Or, perhaps it will start to happen later. Could today have been in some way a beginning for you?

Perhaps you would like to write a letter to God about it, and then imagine yourself posting it through his letter box.

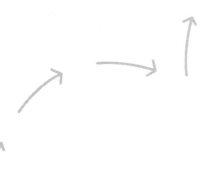

Discovery

Sometimes I receive emails from some unknown recipient who has decided that all and sundry should read this story or joke they have found. Usually such material finds its way quickly into my recycle bin, but this one was different. It made me stop and realize that God does not always open heaven to us in the stereotyped ways that we might think or imagine. The piece is called 'The man and the Butterfly'.

A man was walking through the countryside.

He whispered, 'God speak to me,' and a meadowlark sang.

But the man did not hear.

As the man walked along, storm clouds were gathering.

This time he yelled, 'God speak to me,' and the thunder and lightning rolled across the sky.

But the man did not listen.

Later that night the man looked up into the sky.

He said, 'God let me see you,' and a star shone brightly.

But the man did not see.

Then the man shouted, 'God show me a miracle.'

Down the road a new baby was born.

But the man did not notice.

The next day the man cried, 'God, I need your help.'

An email arrived bringing him some good news.

But the man deleted it and continued crying.

Walking outside in despair he blurted out, 'Touch me, God, and let me know you are here.'

At that moment God reached down and touched the man.

But the man brushed the butterfly off, and walked on.

So, don't miss out, because God isn't packaged the way you expect!

Spiritual Notepad

☆ Before you pack up and go, try and sum up your experience with a few sentences that capture for you the important thoughts and ideas and moments of your day out, if you have not done so already.

☆ Are there any things that you thought you must do or act on, arising out of your reflections today?

☆ Do carry on talking to God and thinking as you retrace your steps and make your way home after this rather special day out.

Checking Out

You can use the guide below to see how you feel after having experienced the *Twelve Days Out with God*. You can then use this to compare with your original answers at the start of the book.

On a scale of 1 to 10, put a ring around where you would consider yourself at the moment in . . .

Your personal day to day relationship with God:

1   2   3   4   5   6   7   8   9   10
Low   High

Your prayer life:

1   2   3   4   5   6   7   8   9   10
Low   High

Your measure of faith and trust:

1   2   3   4   5   6   7   8   9   10
Low   High

Your knowledge of your inner self:

1   2   3   4   5   6   7   8   9   10
Low   High

Your general spiritual fitness:

1   2   3   4   5   6   7   8   9   10
Low   High

Confidence in your ability to get closer to God:

1   2   3   4   5   6   7   8   9   10
Low   High

What areas in your relationship with God would you like to explore more?

_____

_____

_____

_____

_____

_____

_____

_____

_____

_____

_____

_____

_____

_____

_____

_____

_____

_____

_____

_____

So What's Next?

Your journey of discovery does not have to end here. Someone once described God as a diamond. When you hold up one of these precious pieces of glass to the light and slowly turn it, a million different colours suddenly appear. God has so many different facets to his personality yet to discern, and there are so many things that he still wants to do in your life that it's easy to plan many more days out with God.

Acknowledgements

We would like to thank the following people for their help and suggestions in field-testing this book: Claire Cottrell, Pauline Foster, Sue and Dave Howells, Lyn Styles, Alison Ward and Rebecca Elcome.

Special thanks to Senior Acquisitions Editor Amy Boucher Pye for her willingness to listen to the original concept and share its future potential.

Some of the stories, jokes and experiences contained in this book come from a wide range of sources. We have tried to credit wherever possible, but we will be happy to correct our mistakes as necessary in future editions of this book.

We would also like to take this opportunity to thank our wives Caroline Elcome and Trinity Gidney and our families for the encouragement and support they gave in the writing of this book.

An Exciting Series
Featuring Inspirational True-Life Stories

A Long Hot Soak

Edited by Chris Gidney

Softcover: 0-002-74056-7

Another Long Hot Soak
Book Two

Edited by Chris Gidney

Softcover: 0-310-25176-1

Another Long Hot Soak
Book Three

Edited by Chris Gidney

Softcover: 0-310-25177-X

Another Long Hot Soak
Book Four

Edited by Chris Gidney

Softcover: 0-310-25178-8

Pick up a copy at your favourite bookstore!

ZONDERVAN™

GRAND RAPIDS, MICHIGAN 49530 USA

WWW.ZONDERVAN.COM